THE REGIONAL PROBLEM

THE
REGIONAL PROBLEM

Stuart Holland

St. Martin's Press   New York

To Michael Cherniavsky,
with thanks for
teaching me

CONTENTS

PREFACE

This book is about political economy and the regions. It advances some of the main arguments developed in *Capital versus the Regions* (Macmillan, 1976) and relates them to regional policies and problems in Western Europe and the United States.

One of the key themes in the work is the extent to which the main body of regional theory and policy in capitalist countries is divorced from the unequal competition between big-league and small-league firms. In other words, the trend to monopoly and multi-national capital has established a new meso-economic sector between the conventional macro- and micro-economic orthodoxies as displayed in the literature.

Unless governments harness this meso-economic power as the basis for new regional planning they will not be able to transform the present imbalance in the regional distribution of jobs and incomes. Yet the harnessing of meso-economic power represents a major challenge to both liberal capitalist ideology and the modern capitalist state.

State capitalism, through new public enterprise, played a major role in the early regional development of the United States, and has been given new dimensions by some post-war European governments. But state capitalism poses its own problems for the governments which introduce it. It challenges the dominance of private power in the heartland of the modern capitalist economy. For such and other reasons, it is difficult to introduce a radical and effective regional policy without confronting private capitalist power and transcending the limits of state capitalist policies. Only the main parties of the European Left in Britain, France and Italy have real prospects of transforming problem regions in a strategy for wider political and economic transformation.

This argument, and the research behind it, reflects nearly ten years work in regional theory and policy which I have been able to undertake on both sides of the Atlantic.

I am grateful to many people for their patience and help during my researches, and in particular to the Brookings Institution in Washington D.C.; the SVIMEZ Research

Institute in Rome; the Délégation à l'Aménagement du Territoire (DATAR) in Paris; and to the Centre for Contemporary European Studies in Sussex, where I held a Research Fellowship for three years.

I am also grateful to Tibor Barna, Stephen Drewer, John Myerscough and Ray Thomas for reading all or part of the text. Naturally, they are not responsible for the arguments which it contains.

I particularly would like to add some words on the man to whom this book is dedicated: Michael Cherniavsky. Michael not only was an exceptional Head of the History Department at Christ's Hospital, who ensured that successive pupils there went on to university, but he also embodied with elements of genius what one could call the Rousseau approach to education – literally leading us out of childhood into intellectual adolescence, rather than imposing a particular view of either history or the world. For this, as well as for a grounding in scholarship which I may or may not have fulfilled, I owe him a debt which cannot be fully repaid.

Throughout the text the abbreviations M.D.R. and L.D.R. have been used for more-developed and less-developed regions.

European School   STUART HOLLAND
University of Sussex

CHAPTER 1

POLITICS, ECONOMICS AND REGIONS

According to much regional theory there should be no regional problem. Its premises assume a harmonious self-adjustment in an idealised capitalist system. They maintain that if companies took work to where labour was most available while labour also migrated to where work could be found, everything would balance out. In such a way disparities in profits, wages and employment between different regions would be merely frictional. The resulting society might still be subject to class divisions between organised capital and organised labour, but social class divisions would not be aggravated by regional differentials in employment and income.

Clearly something is wrong with the theory, the system, or both. It needs very little to observe that modern capitalist economies have not fulfilled the premises of such a self-adjusting and self-balancing regional model. On the other hand, there is disagreement whether this constitutes a regional problem. For one thing, this will depend on who you are, where you live, whether you are employed and what your income prospects are. One school of thought maintains that uneven development between regions is essential to the dynamic growth of a capitalist system, and that the attempt to secure greater regional equality through government redistribution policies reduces the over-all level of income to be distributed. Another, largely represented by private enterprise and its trade associations, maintains that capitalist firms are rational in their location decisions (when government allows them to decide for themselves) and that workers are not. Alternatively, it holds that firms locate where their receipts and profits are highest, while workers who choose not to migrate thereby maximise non-economic gains. It also maintains that workers who resist the closure of plant in problem regions are hurting themselves in the long run through reducing the over-all level of income in the economy.[1]

This version of the 'take up thy bed and walk' philosophy has become increasingly hard to reconcile with major and *persistent* disparities in the regional distribution of employment; related disparities in the rate of growth of regional product and productivity; regional differences in activity rates and the under-utilisation of the national labour force; congestion in areas of labour inflow and involuntary unemployment in labour-outflow areas, plus a wide range of disparities in the provision and utilisation of social services in different regions. There is increasing evidence to support the claim that such disparities in large part arise from the workings of a capitalist system in which private companies are not obliged to face the social costs of their location decisions and in which governments for a variety of reasons find it difficult to compel them to do so.

On the other hand, it is important to distinguish between regional disparities which arise because of the workings of capitalism, and those which arise because of other factors. For instance, up to four-fifths of industrial investment in both East and West Europe (therefore including the Comecon countries) takes the form of replacement investment in existing plant and facilities.[2] This proportion might be lowered by better forward planning of investment and location, releasing more for location in persistent low-employment areas, but it still means that much investment will occur where it has already taken place unless governments close down establishments in already more developed regions, in which case they will meet local resistance in either capitalist or socialist systems. The Yugoslavs have found this in their socialist market economy in which worker-controlled companies have mainly been free to choose where their next new plant should be located. Also, even if there is a wide range of choice between no locational controls at all and controls of the Stalinist type, the political costs of total central control of location in either a socialist or capitalist economy may be unacceptable to most of the working population, especially if the controls include the restriction of voluntary labour migration.

These issues are taken up in the concluding chapter of this book. But at the outset it may be worth pointing out that even in an equal incomes and full-employment economy, where the government guaranteed income equality through tax transfers and guaranteed full employment by keeping everyone in some kind of job, there would still be a trend to regional disparities in terms of product, productivity and income to firms. These would tend to be cumulative, raising the interregional income transfer obligations on the government, unless offset by regional development policies. For instance, a region which had failed to adapt an outdated industrial structure to modern products and techniques would be producing goods more expensively than a region which had succeeded in such adaptation. Therefore over-all productivity in the national economy would be lower to the extent that the problem region had failed to adapt and modernise. Inversely, real welfare for the economy as a whole would be reduced to the extent that resources were being employed in congested regions on projects such as housing, hospitals, schools and urban roads which in less congested regions would cost less. Also, the persistence of an outdated agricultural structure in regions which could raise output per head through modernisation or industrialisation means that the economy and society as a whole would secure a lower over-all income for equal distribution than if such a structure was redeveloped.

In response to such a case for regional development it is sometimes maintained that economic welfare has little to do with welfare as such; that happiness is not measured in the percentage increase of regional or national productivity, and that modernisation has its own social costs.[3] In other words, it is claimed that we should preserve regional differences in life style, and especially preserve non-industrial areas. It would be unjust simply to claim that most of those in favour of preserving rural areas are middle-class professionals who want to fossilise the character of their weekend retreats. Similarly the environmentalist lobby is not wholly composed of the super-rich, even if it notably lacks both the unskilled and the unemployed. On the other hand, there is a difference between the weekend retreat from industrial society of the middle classes who can afford it, and the retreat of industry from working-class people who are involuntarily unemployed in a declining region. Also, the choice of dropping out for the individual who could earn a good living from professional skills is different from the lack of choice for the industrial worker who is forced to drop his work, skills and earnings by adaptation problems which his local employer has failed to overcome. The quality of life may be less measurable the higher we take it. For instance, how much is subsidised opera worth in purely economic terms? But the quality of life which is forgone by the regionally unemployed can be directly measured in terms of personal income forgone, and indirectly indicated in terms of lost output and earnings to the economy as a whole, which has its own feedback on how many opera subsidies or other varieties of social expenditure we can afford.

National and International Regions

The definition of regions is a game which can be played with almost infinite variations. Geographers had a head start on regional economists, and placed faith for a long time in what was called a 'natural' region. This was an area in which many physical and human factors interacted to form a part of geographical space which was recognisably different and distinctive from others. But they found that different characteristics gave rise to different regional boundaries.[4] In other words, a natural region might be defined in terms of particular homogeneous characteristics, but not all the characteristics conveniently overlapped in such a way as to isolate the region from all others. One way round this was to consider the region *as if* it were isolated in such a way, and to consider what would happen to it if it were. A supplementary method was to consider a region in terms of only a few homogeneous characteristics, such as the market area and the influence of a small number of firms and industries, and to consider their interrelationship with each other rather than their interrelationship with other firms outside the region. Regional theory tended for some time to concentrate upon the location characteristics of firms in relation to labour, raw materials and transport costs, with the result that the kind of 'region' concerned in such analysis could be very small. Also, its use in analysis could be highly artificial, neglecting the interrelationships between it and other regions elsewhere. In economic terms such regional theory amounted to a spatial dimension of the conventional theory of the firm – or micro-economics.

Between the First and Second World Wars two economists

broke away from this micro-economic definition of regions and established a more macro-economic framework which considered not only the internal characteristics of national sub-regions, but also the relationship of these regions with the rest of the national and international economy. Bertil Ohlin used the term 'region' to mean not only a particular geographical area, but also an area in which the proportions of labour and capital showed particular characteristics which distinguished it from other areas, either national or international.[5] Basically, Ohlin worked down to national regions from the level of international trade theory, rather than up from the theory of the location of the firm. His work both widened the use of the term 'region' and advanced on some of the conventional international trade theory of his time, although it remained within the then orthodox assumption of a long-run equilibrium or self-adjustment in the employment of capital and labour through the free working of the market mechanism.

The other economist who broke away from the restricted localised use of the term 'region', Lucien Brocard, is less well known than Ohlin, but opened up the approach to regional theory and analysis which was later to become identified with François Perroux. Basically, Brocard worked up from the spatial implications of micro-economics to interregional and international macro-economics. His analysis widened interrelated areas: (1) local; (2) regional; (3) national; and (4) international. He had a clear idea of his own methodology, writing that

> to tackle the problem of human co-operation by the study of international co-operation is like wanting to begin a building with the roof or the top floor. Tackling the problem with the study of national co-operation, as the theorists of the national economy have done to date, is to build by starting with the first floor. Our method is to begin with the foundations, which are the regional and local economy.[6]

Brocard's methodology also differed from Ohlin's inasmuch as he considered the spatial distribution of activity to represent a process of continual and asymmetrical disequilibrium rather than equilibrium or self-balance.

Two first-rank post-war economists – Perroux and Myrdal – shared Brocard's methodology in considering national and international regions as different but related dimensions of spatial distribution, and in their emphasis on disequilibrium or unbalance in such distribution. Myrdal's main work on regional theory appeared after Perroux's earliest articles and seems to have been independent of them.[7] Both authors have made a major contribution to drawing the attention of governments and international authorities to common factors in national and international regional economics.

Since the late 1950s Myrdal has increasingly concerned himself with the problem of international regions of which the major study on Asia is the most notable example.[8] He has also pioneered analysis of regional problems in international economic integration, such as the European Economic Community and the Latin American Free Trade Area.[9] Such international areas tend to share two main characteristics: (1) some homogeneity of economic structure and level of development, at least in relation to other international regions, and (2) geographical contiguity or proximity. The homogeneity is relative. Latin American economies include wide national and sub-national variations in the structure of production and the distribution of income and employment. Also, their geographical proximity does not mean that they are economically proximate, because of the possibility of geographical obstacles to trade such as the Andes range in South America, and because of economic links in trade with more developed economies outside the area. But it is in such senses that the term 'international region' tends to be used by international organisations such as the United Nations.

Like Myrdal, Perroux has shown a clear awareness of the international dimension of regional problems and has stressed that the nation state is but one unit in a wider regional and international distribution of resources and activity. But initially he developed a typology of national sub-regions which became an orthodoxy both in France and elsewhere. As early as 1950 Perroux wrote that it was important to advance economic analysis from what he called an 'abstract' or 'banal' concept of space, and to define different dimensions of economic space. These included: (1) statistically uniform or 'homogeneous' space; (2) space as a *champ de forces* or area of specific economic factors; and (3) planned space, or space as an area in which certain policy decisions are supposed to be implemented.[10] In later writing this initial definition of space was translated into three categories of region: (1) homogeneous regions; (2) polarised regions; and (3) planning regions.[11] In fact, the first and third categories differ from the second. They do not necessarily imply economic interpretation, or theory, rather than statistical definition. The 'homogeneous' region shares the same aims and the same limits as the 'natural' region of geographers; its homogeneous characteristics may have different boundaries, depending on their extent in space. The 'planning' region is the easiest to determine, since for obvious reasons most governments which have concerned themselves with regional planning or development policies have designated regions in terms of already existing administrative areas for which they have statistical information.

In many ways it is the 'polarised' region or the region as *champ de forces* which is the most interesting of Perroux's concepts, precisely because it represents a theory of regional behaviour and activity. It advances on the equilibrium or self-balancing assumptions of earlier economic theory of spatial distribution, and shares a higher explanatory value of the nature of regional disequilibria with Myrdal's work. But in statistical terms, the 'polarised' region is difficult to measure. The process of polarisation is basically the attraction of factors of activity to certain points in space in a manner similar to magnetic polarisation. But, as with the description of 'homogeneous' regions, the description of the factors involved in polarisation tends to entail different boundaries for different factors. Boudeville has tried to show polarisation in terms of population density, and the French regional planning authorities have drawn up a variety of indices which give a good visual impression of the degree of polarisation in various areas of France both to date and as anticipated up to the year 2000.[12] But the polarised factors do not conveniently coincide with administrative or planning regions. Moreover, this is not simply through inertia on the part of administrators, but because the reorganisation of administrative regions on contemporary polarisation indices not only would have to draw on past data (which would only be possible on the basis of administrative areas in any case), but would not necessarily coincide with the future polarisation pattern, which, by nature, will tend to change over time.

For these reasons, plus the fact that changing the basis of data collection tends to make comparison over time much more difficult (unless one continually duplicates both the old and the new data collection), governments tend to use existing administrative areas for regional accounting. This does not prevent them from dividing such areas into qualitatively different categories, but these tend to be limited by the geographical boundaries of the administrative areas concerned. Simply, this means that an area which includes different characteristics will tend to be included under the heading of the predominant feature. Thus a relatively developed region may include major pockets of persistent unemployment, but none the less be categorised as 'developed'. Inversely, a relatively less developed region may include high employment and income centres, yet be described over-all as 'undeveloped'. This might seem mere semantics, but in fact the designation of regions by broad categories tends to imply that – over-all – they are eligible or ineligible for a particular development-assistance package. In other words, governments which only make such broad categories may be helping enterprise, income and employment in some thriving areas while doing nothing to reduce persistent unemployment in others. So the definition of different types of region is of considerable importance, especially when they are based on administrative units which have not themselves been designed for regional statistics or policy.

Most modern capitalist governments have evolved a more sophisticated degree of definition for different regions than the simple division into 'developed' and 'undeveloped'. A sample range in Western Europe or the United States would not include all of the following definitions, but would include some of them by the same or similar names:

(1) *over-developed regions,* in which the process of development has given rise to measurable congestion costs and pressures on existing or new infrastructure, which can only be provided at higher cost and loss of amenity than elsewhere in the economy;

(2) *neutral regions,* in which there are high levels of employment and income but no marked congestion costs or pressures. Such regions may well operate as satellites to over-developed or

congested regions, and constitute a belt or band around a major metropolitan area;

(3) *intermediate regions*, in which there is a mixed pattern of employment and income distribution, and a combination of some of the features of more developed and less developed areas, including major pockets of persistent unemployment of the kind already outlined;

(4) *depressed regions*, in which the rate or level of development has failed to match the rest of the national economy and shows no signs of alignment with it. Such regions classically include a concentration of industries (textiles, shipbuilding and, until recently, coal) in which employment has been in relative or absolute decline;

(5) *under-developed regions*, or regions in which modern industrial capitalism has never developed on any scale. These are mainly agricultural regions with peasant smallholdings or small capitalist farms, and in many cases are sparsely populated with few or no major urban settlements.

The Urban–Regional Interface

As geographers realise very well, the level of development of a region is to some extent associated with its degree and structure of urbanisation. For instance, to parallel the definition of different types of region just given, an *over-developed* region probably will include a major metropolis, or a Perroux 'growth pole' which has become 'critical'; *neutral* regions may be characterised by a new town satellite belt; *intermediate* regions may include a combination of thriving and declining urban areas, *depressed* regions tend to include a concentration of old urban structures dating from the Industrial Revolution which have not been able to adapt or modernise in the twentieth century; *under-developed* regions either lack major urban settlements or have few industrialised or modern service centres. But while such a parallel listing of features is tempting, it can also become too simple and hence misleading. For instance, major congested or over-developed regions may include a 'downtown' core in which unskilled employment or total employment is declining, and share some of the characteristics of urban areas in depressed regions. On the other hand, such core areas will tend to include high rent and income development in dense office development and upper-income flats or housing, segmented with parcels or belts of what amounts to slum housing. In other words, even the urban core may not have a conveniently homogeneous composition. But, in general, the urban dimension to the regional problem is crucial in understanding what the problem is really about, particularly since urban areas already include from one-half to two-thirds of the population in Western European countries, three-quarters of the population in Canada, and four-fifths of the population in the United States.[13]

This trend to urbanisation clearly raises the question whether urban problems do not justify a theory of urban economics independently of regional economic theory. In fact, the urban–regional interface both is more general and more important than many urban physical planners have until recently been prepared to admit. Urban physical planning has its special problems, demanding skills and decision-making which are not commonly available to both regional economists and urban planners, despite the fact that the increasing spread of combined regional–urban studies courses in universities is reducing the communication barriers between economists and architects, land-use planners and similarly interested groups. The interface has also been to a certain extent confused in countries such as Britain in the late 1960s by the fact that Regional Economic Planning Councils were established which in practice had few or no economic responsibilities (which remained primarily with central government) and were almost exclusively concerned with physical land-use planning. This gave rise to a marked disenchantment with regional economic planning as such, and a tendency to re-assert philosophies of urban planning which neglected either the economic base of urban areas or their interrelationship with other urban and non-urban regions in the economy.

One of the clearest respects in which the urban–regional interface can be shown is interregional labour migration. The demand for immigrant labour in pressured urban areas influences the national pattern of labour demand as well as wage and price levels. To the extent that management in urban labour-inflow areas is able to pass on increased wage costs through its price-making or price-leadership position, the relative urban scarcity in accommodation will mean higher wage demands than otherwise would have occurred through the location of plant in less-pressured regions. And this will mean a greater loss to national export competitiveness than would have occurred through expansion of the less-pressured regions. But the costs and benefits of cumulative labour inflow to high-demand urban areas also influence the case for a national regional policy on other grounds. On the benefit side there is the highly disputed question whether urban areas of a particular minimum size are necessary for the provision of both external services and essential supplies to firms which could not otherwise produce and sell efficiently. This issue underlies the whole concentration and dispersion debate in national locational policy, including whether there is a case for Perroux-type growth centres in development areas. On the cost side, the unrestrained high density development of the main urban areas of labour inflow not only may make them uninhabitable for all save green-belt commuters, but impose larger social capital expenditure – especially in traffic control and new road network expenditure – than would obtain in less-developed regions.

There are other respects, in which the urban and regional problems are woven (or knotted) in the same fabric. For instance, 'export base' theory makes specifically economic assumptions about the adjustment of producers to changing export demand patterns. But it has mainly been applied – with reason – to the economic base of urban areas where most export employment will be concentrated. This theory has been employed in the context of self-sustaining stages of growth theory, with the assumption that the urban base will be able to adjust over the long term to changes in export markets and opportunities elsewhere in the national economy.[14] But it also has been challenged in terms of Myrdal's 'backwash' theory, which maintains that an area which loses export competitiveness towards other areas may thereby also lose the capital, the skilled labour and the management which had made the initial exports possible, undermining the base which would be necessary to secure a successful export adjustment.[15] The catalogue of stranded shipbuilding, textiles or coal-mining areas in most mature capitalist economies which lend support to the Myrdalian hypothesis are principally *urban* areas composing larger administrative or homogeneous regions, even if their adaptation problems concern the wider interregional employment of factors of production and trade in the national and international economy. Similarly, even successful urban export areas in the national economy may include the kind of central area unemployment and failed adaptation to which reference has already been made. Any resolution of their problems must consider the case for providing more diversified modern employment opportunities. For major urban areas such as Greater London, which is about the population size of Sweden, this diversification not only should mean consideration of the inter-sectoral composition of local production, but also national and international long-term changes in the sectoral composition of demand.

These are issues which should be seen as both regional *and* urban in character. Even the problems of agricultural regions, which remain substantial on the Continent of Europe and in the United States, cannot be isolated from the urban problem at a national level. For instance, in the United States the urban crisis as officially recognised by state and federal officials includes the continuous swelling of the pool of urban unemployed through out-migration from the problem rural regions of Appalachia and the Deep South. In the U.S. case, the problem is partly intractable precisely because it is treated more as an urban than an interregional problem.[16] Independently of any escape from racism in the South, the northwards flow into the urban unemployment pool is not likely to ebb until both social security and employment levels in or near the initial rural outflow areas compare with those in the North as a whole. Social security benefits are particularly important in the New York case, yet again demonstrate how an introverted urban policy – however well-intentioned – cannot readily neglect the interregional income transfers which would be necessary to prevent a greater regional migration than the northern urban areas can cope with.

Regional Inequality as the Regional Problem

One reason for maintaining that regional inequalities constitute a problem is the question of national costs in the imbalanced use of regional resources. In simple terms, there is a loss of output and income to the national economy from the over-development of leading regions and the under-development of others. The accounting of such problems as yet has hardly begun.[17] And this is substantially because the dominant self-balance school in much regional theory has acted as an obstacle to the identification of the costs of imbalanced resource use. In terms of its own assumptions of a perfectly self-adjusting capitalist system, such costs can only arise because of frictions or imperfections in the long-run working of the market. They are seen as exceptions rather than the rule. For this reason, much of this theory has been preoccupied with evolving theoretical models of self-adjustment, which have a high social cost in themselves detracting resources from regional cost–benefit accounting.

It is hoped that criticism of such self-adjustment mythology will help reverse this imbalance in regional economics. And this means the need for a theoretical attack on the self-balance case to show its own intellectual bankruptcy. Facts on regional inequalities in themselves prove little. They can only be used to show the costs of regional imbalance in a theoretical context which explains the role of inequalities in imposing costs on society as a whole. Besides, partly because of the dominance of the nation state, data collection at the regional level tends to be mediocre. For instance, Italy and Japan are the only two countries in the world which keep systematic and highly disaggregated data on regional product or value added per head. The European Economic Community has made marginal progress in trying to collate statistics which are comparable between member countries, but so far has made little progress in industry disaggregation of product per head. This is crucial, since such data shows the underlying structural disparities between regions at the level of the firm and industry. They are an X-ray through the aggregate figures on income per head by region, which alone can help us really understand how extensive the regional imbalance in resource use can be.

Disaggregation of regional data such as are available from some national accounts statistics and specialised studies is used in relation to the theoretical argument through this text. A survey of the pattern of regional inequalities in the six original member countries of the E.E.C., plus Britain, is given in Chapter

5. However, as an opener on the importance of regional disparities, two main observations can be made.

First, as one of the main British regional studies recently put it, 'the benefits of interregional equalisation are small in comparison with the benefits of complete equalisation of incomes'. For instance, inter-industry wage differentials in Britain are as much as three times aggregate interregional differentials in income. The same study made a hypothetical calculation that the proportionate gain from equalising incomes between two regional communities – with incomes in the one originally 20 per cent higher than in the other – would amount to only about 2 per cent of the gain from a complete equalisation of personal incomes.[18] As the study admits, this is playing theoretical games, at least to the extent that a precise figure is given to the outcome. In practical political terms, the equalisation game may of course be serious, and lead to breaking the rules of the existing system. The important perspective to gain on such calculations runs mainly as follows: first, the distribution of personal income in most modern capitalist economies is massively weighted in the favour of a small minority of the total population who control the bulk of personal wealth. In Britain 2 per cent of the population account for 80 per cent of the personally held shares in the economy, and income from these shares enters in post-tax income.[19] Expressed differently, the comparative argument from inter-personal income inequality reinforces the case for abolishing the privileged economic base of the 2 per cent minority, rather than weakening the case for regional equalisation. Secondly, a very high proportion of the total population in most modern capitalist economies spend their lives in regions or areas which have major differences in income per head, job opportunities, social environment, and general opportunity. In other words, regional disparities tend to be smaller than inter-personal disparities, but they affect many more people because of the less concentrated extremes. Thirdly, the failure to assure a balanced regional employment of resources can act as a major restraint on the rate of growth of national income, and mean the loss of absolute income gains because of relative regional disparities.[20]

The question of absolute and relative gains throws light on the second main observation worth making at this stage on the meaning of regional inequalities. A study undertaken by the E.E.C. Commission has shown that in some of the main member countries such as France and Belgium the metropolitan centre regions such as Brussels and Paris have massively increased their lead on other areas of the country in terms of income or product per head. But it has also shown that the absolute percentage growth of income necessary for backward regions to catch up with leading regions is massively higher than anything achieved in Community countries to date. Taking a fifteen-year period and a national or Community growth rate of 4 per cent a year, it would be necessary for a region with one-half of the leading region's income level to grow by 9 per cent a year to catch up, and a region with one-third of the highest level 12 per cent a year. The rates rise to 11 per cent and 14 per cent respectively if the average growth of the national or Community economy is 6 per cent rather than 4 per cent. Such growth rates are way above those achieved by even the fastest growing areas of the European Community in recent years. On the other hand, the scale of interregional disparities in the Community is very real. The Community regions with less than one-half of the income per head of the leading region (Paris) include even the developed areas of Piedmont and Liguria in the North of Italy, while most of the regions in the South of Italy have income per head levels less than one-quarter that of Paris.[21]

Politics and the Regional Problem

There is little doubt that what has come to be recognised as 'the regional problem' arose more from political pressure to redress such regional disparities than from any insight by professional economists. And there is nothing illegitimate about this. For one thing, the professional economist's attention to regional problems mainly followed political awareness that a problem existed in the first place. Also, as is suggested towards the end of this chapter, many professional economists have been concerned with idealised models of spatial distribution rather than regional problems in the economies in which they live. If either admission or analysis of the problem had been left to economists alone we still might be in a meta-regional wonderland. On the other hand, there is little unanimity of opinion among politicians either about what constitutes a regional problem, or which policies might be pursued to cope with it. Also, if a politician is doing his job properly, his own views will depend partly on personal and professional insight, but also on the pressures for or against regional policy from those whom he represents. The politicians representing higher-income classes in developed areas may tend to play down the need for regional policy, while those representing the unemployed in, say Clydeside, Sardinia or Appalachia, will tend to press the case for it.

The reflection of different interests in this way is not surprising in countries which have developed democratic representative institutions. But the successful representation of the views of the regionally under-privileged will depend on their strength in representing their interests to governments, or their organised bargaining strength through extra-parliamentary action. The degree of centralisation in the governments of some of the main Western European economies has resulted in separatist groups resorting to direct action to achieve outside the representative framework what they have failed to secure within it. Besides, governments in general choose between different priorities as they see them. They may simply fail to grasp the fact that there is a crucial interdependence between regional and national economic development. Thus they may put the balance of payments, or inflation, or the promotion of national industrial investment before more intensive measures to cope with the regional problem without appreciating the extent to which the under-utilisation of labour in a problem region and the transmission of congestion costs in pressured regions into higher producer prices intensifies the national policy problems to which they are giving a spurious priority.

In other words, even if governments frequently have anti-cipated professional economists in appreciating that something must be done about regional problems, they do not necessarily know either what should be done, or how it relates to the rest of what they are doing. It is in these respects that economic analysis of regional interrelationships is crucial to the formulation of policies capable of coping with the problems which politicians broadly perceive. It includes analyses of the role of the modern capitalist state as *umpire* (the rules of the game in dealing with leading firms, and the choice of particular national and regional policies); as *regulator* of government expenditure and its regional composition; as *entrepreneur,* deciding on the regional distribution of public enterprise; and as *planner,* in the sense of formalised forward policy-maker for the national and regional economies.[22]

The over-all posture which the State will adopt in these various respects depends much more explicitly than many regional economists are prepared to admit on the class nature of its political support. One does not have to be a Marxist to see the force of this case. It can be seen in the extent to which some governments are elected on the basis of major contributions from organised business and some on major contributions from organised labour. If this were the end of the issue it might not amount to much. But, in practice, it amounts to much more. For one thing, even a government elected against the vociferous opposition of organised business may find or imagine itself obliged to placate the 'business community' in such a way that it does not implement policies which would offend that community but which would help problem regions. For instance, inasmuch as the potential flow of direct investment from more to less developed regions depends on the availability of entirely new and potentially 'footloose' plant (mainly in modern manufacturing and 'head-office' services), no inflow of directly productive investment and employment through such plant can be organised without either maintaining or increasing the rate of national investment. But the advent of a left-wing government may prompt private management in these sectors to adopt a defensive 'wait-and-see' attitude towards investment in the home market, or accelerate direct foreign investment. It will wait to see what kind of umpire the new government proves to be; where and to whom it allocates government expenditure; whether it favours state versus private entrepreneurs; and whether its regional planning amounts to anything more than the statement of Panglossian intentions which private enterprise trade associations could have published. If the government shows its teeth, the large-scale private sector may harden its defensive non-co-operative position and hope that the government will neglect those parts of its programme which entail any change in the status quo for private enterprise.

To the extent that private enterprise dominates modern

manufacturing and mobile services, which are essential for those sectors bringing employment opportunities into the regions, and to the extent that its defensive 'wait-and-see' posture results in either a deteriorating trade balance, or a run on the currency reserves, or both, the national government may capitulate in terms of the extent to which it intended to base its regional policy on investment by leading national or multi-national firms. This may show itself in a variety of ways, depending on the type of regional policy already adopted or proposed. For instance, if government controls over the location of extensions to new plant have already been introduced – such as the British Industrial Development Certificates policy – the government either may relax the area of new factory space to which they apply, or maintain or reduce the area to which they apply but, in practice, fail to enforce it with any rigour for balance-of-payments or other macro-economic reasons. Alternatively, for fear of depressing national investment levels, it may hesitate to extend public enterprise into modern manufacturing and services in such a way as to give it a complement of firms across the broad range of 'footloose' enterprise, capable of making a direct contribution to regional development.

As later chapters argue in detail, the role of locational controls and public enterprise are crucial tests of the readiness of governments in modern capitalist economies to tackle the regional problem with any seriousness. This is basically because they are the key *direct* policy instruments within the national government's armoury, as opposed to *indirect* policy measures of the incentives and infrastructure improvement variety. That is to say, they are policies which are obligatory for the companies concerned, and which thereby reduce the element of uncertainty in fulfilling regional development targets. But they are interdependent. The failure of leading private enterprise to undertake that rate of investment which will produce new plant capable of location in problem regions may demand that the State take over those companies which fail to fulfil such growth. Private enterprise will wait to see whether the government will take up the challenge, which certainly would amount to an alteration of the 'rules of the game' in most capitalist economies other than Italy, where public enterprise, organised in holding companies, has secured an extensive grip on modern manufac-

turing and services.[23] At the same time the electorate of the
nation's problem regions will wait to see whether the national
government is going to deliver the new employment opportunities which in their own eyes are certainly due to them.

If the government fails to deliver the new employment it can
hardly be surprised that the regions should persuade themselves
that their best hope of coping effectively with their problems is
political self-determination, and that organised separatist movements of the kind seen in Brittany, Scotland and Wales should
arise. Nor should they be surprised at the resort to violence
between Walloons and Flemings in Belgium (where cultural
differences are reinforced by regional economic disparities
between the Walloon and Flemish regions); in Northern Ireland
(traditionally by far the poorest region in the United Kingdom);
or Calabria (the poorest region in Italy).

But the resort to direct action may not assure separatist
movements either political independence or an increase in their
economic welfare. For one thing, governments may well feel
that they can 'ride out the storm' without loss to their national
political base, which may be concentrated in the more prosperous regions which possess a majority of the voting population.
Alternatively, the government may decide that the political
problems are so intractable that it should grant the region
autonomy either on a partial or total basis. But in the case of
Northern Ireland a regional government not only failed to
represent the interest of its own permanent minority in such a
way as to avoid an emerging civil war, but was not in a position to
secure an equalisation of its own employment and income levels
with the rest of the British economy. Even the attainment of
political independence and the establishment of a separate
currency, as in the case of the Republic of Eire, may not mean a
rapid increase in economic welfare if the newly autonomous
nation state remains effectively 'integrated' into the economy of
which it was previously a subsidiary region.

Economic Theory as a Regional Problem

As with the economic problems of national sub-regions,
economists should be able to help politicians to clarify the
implications from such federalist regional structures as at-

tempted in the United States, and now proposed for the E.E.C.
But, so far, relatively little attention has been paid by regional
economists to the economic factors in regional political problems. Moreover, either through the artificial nature of their
assumptions or through a partial approach to general problems,
many economists have handicapped rather than helped regional
policy-makers. The artificial assumptions have become part of
the regional problem in the sense that they have acted as an
obstacle to perception of the multi-dimensional and interrelated
features of uneven development in modern capitalist economies.

One of the main reasons why regional theory has itself
become a regional problem stems from the fact that classical
economic theory was hardly concerned with regional problems,
and that neo-classical regional analysis chose to marry the
economics of a perfect or idealised model of competition in a
capitalist economy to idealised geographical models of the
spatial distribution of activity. In other words, neo-classical
economic theory, which has constituted the bulk of the regional
theory emerging from the United States since 1945, has taken its
point of departure from artificial premises, rather than from the
more realistic premises of the main classical economists who
became aware during the nineteenth century of the divorce
between their economic theories and social, economic and
political realities. Some of the leading exponents, such as Walter
Isard, have attempted to advance beyond regional economics
into social and political issues. But they did so by applying a
utilitarian calculus which in key respects assumed equality of
opportunity of precisely the kind which regional inequality
prevents.[24]

In general, this work is an attempt to de-mystify the regional
problem through a critique of the orthodoxies which have
increasingly perplexed students and which have been rejected in
favour of 'rule-of-thumb' measures by policy-makers. It has
extensive political implications, mainly because it analyses the
regional problem as endemic to the working of the market
mechanism in the modern capitalist economy.

CHAPTER 2

CAPITALISM AND REGIONAL IMBALANCE

Capitalism cannot be defined simply by reference to a free-market mechanism. The market mechanism has been employed to varying degrees in socialist economies as a means of indicating social and economic preferences in resource use. One of the key differences between capitalist and socialist systems is the ownership and control of the surplus produced by the system over and above current consumption needs.

In a free-market economy of the kind hypothesised in most regional theory, capitalist management is free to choose the location of this surplus in the form of new investment. This is the spatial dimension of a wider freedom which includes the choice whether to retain a given proportion of the generated surplus for future investment, or to dispose of it to shareholders in the form of distributed profits. Capitalist theory of regional location assumes that private enterprise will follow a cost-minimisation policy in choosing the location of new investment. The 'purer' versions of the theory go further and assume that the firm will seek to maximise profits, at least over the long run.

Capital versus Labour Migration

At the aggregate interregional level, such theory maintains that private enterprise will inform itself on the structure of costs and benefits in alternative locations. It will locate in areas of high labour availability and low labour cost if the savings in production costs which these represent at least offset the additional transport costs to main markets which increased distance from an original location will entail.

Inversely, it assumes that labour will migrate between regions in response to differences in employment prospects and income levels. This migration of labour from regions of high unemployment and low income will complement the reverse flow of

capital into the labour-outflow regions. The theory maintains
that such a process will continue to the point at which
interregional income and employment are equalised, subject to
'frictions' in the working of the market process. Such self-
balance assumptions underlie virtually all the work published by
the Regional Science Association in the United States, and most
notably that of Walter Isard. A critique of self-balance theory in
relation to the regional growth of the United States is
undertaken in Chapter 6.

According to the theory, this complementary process of
labour and capital flows will partly substitute for interregional
trade. Firms will find it more profitable to locate production in
regions to which they previously exported. The main qualifying
features of this analysis would be (1) *product differentiation,*
whereby the same firm produced different products in different
regions, and (2) *regional specialisation* based on differences in
natural resource endowments (mining, forestry, and so on).

This process of self-balance in regional employment and
income is fictitious and fails to correspond with the observable
features of persistent inequalities in regional income and
employment. The fiction arises both from failure to adjust the
theory to facts, and from false premises in the theory itself which
prevent recognition of the regional imbalance and unequal
development in capitalist economic growth. By the same token,
the refutation of regional self-balance theory can be expressed
in empirical *and* theoretical terms.

For instance, in a two-region economy where regional
population is equal but employment significantly unequal, it can
be expected that some labour will migrate to the full-
employment region from the region where unemployment or
under-employment exist. But, in practice, it is likely that the rate
of growth of income and the rate of profit on capital in the
full-employment region will be higher than in the region of
labour outflow. This will partly relate to the level of income in
the two regions. Income will be higher in the full-employment
region. Larger markets made possible through this income will
mean relatively more capital investment over a wider range of
products than in the less fully employed region.[1]

In separate economies without labour or capital migration
such capital investment could be curtailed through labour

shortage. But in an 'open' national economy with interregional labour migration, labour moving from the lower-employment region to the full-employment region can raise the latter's 'full-employment ceiling'. This means that the rate of regional investment can be maintained over and above what otherwise would have been possible, and a trade or business cycle downturn avoided. Labour immigration from the 'reserve' in the less fully employed region will also tend to restrain the rate of cost-push inflation, or rising labour costs, which otherwise could have occurred.[2]

By this process the labour reserve of the less-developed region (L.D.R.) becomes the lever for new capital accumulation over the long term in the more developed region (M.D.R.). The new investment will embody available technical progress in new product and process innovations, raising productivity, thereby raising the rate of return on capital. In turn this will attract capital in the form of savings from the L.D.R., which now will become both a capital and labour donor to the M.D.R. In this way the M.D.R. will grow at the expense of the L.D.R. Even a relative fall of savings in the latter would deplete its capacity to respond to the capital expansion of the M.D.R. But, in practice, savings will tend to fall both relatively to the M.D.R. and to previous L.D.R. levels. Unless counterbalancing mechanisms engage, the absolute savings level of the L.D.R. may fall.

According to self-adjustment theory, the simultaneous migration of M.D.R. capital to the L.D.R. in the form of direct investment in the region should perform such a counterbalancing role.[3] But even in the limited framework of a two-region economy, this is unlikely to occur. First, replacement investment for outdated plant and equipment in the M.D.R. will account for a high proportion of total new investment. In the post-war capitalist economies this proportion was as high as two-thirds to four-fifths of total investment in the 1950s and the early 1960s.[4] Secondly, labour immigration to the M.D.R. will offset the need to move plant to the L.D.R. in order to secure labour for the expanded investment. Thirdly, the embodiment of technical progress in new process innovation will tend to be relatively capital-intensive, thereby decreasing the relative need for labour as a factor of production in the M.D.R. over the long run. Fourthly, M.D.R. labour needs in manufacturing may also be met in an initial expansionary phase through the reduction of under-employment or technological displacement of labour in other sectors in the M.D.R. economy (agriculture, mining, shipbuilding, and so on).[5]

Imbalanced Growth and Trade

These arguments can be expressed in Marxist terms. For instance, they are paralleled by Marx's analysis of the reserve army of labour as a lever of capital accumulation, and the rising organic composition of capital or the displacement of labour by capital in the expansionary departments (or sectors) of industry.[6] But they also can be expressed and extended in Keynesian terms using the concepts of Harrod's contribution to the dynamics of capitalist growth. For instance, Keynes's analysis in *The General Theory* showed that capitalist growth without offsetting state intervention was inherently unstable. A recessionary trend in a national economy would be reinforced by both multiplier and accelerator effects. As income growth fell off in particular markets, firms would cut back investment projects, orders from other firms, and the labour and wages paid. This would further depress income through the economy, which would fall in a vicious downwards spiral.[7] Myrdal's contribution to regional economics in the mid-1950s was in large part an extension of these mechanisms of cumulative causation to a regional context – the 'backwash' effect.[8]

Harrod's analysis can be applied to the theory of imbalanced regional growth as soon as it is admitted that labour inflow from the L.D.R. can raise the full-employment ceiling of the M.D.R. In his terminology this operates through two main mechanisms: the 'natural' and the 'warranted' growth rate. The natural growth rate is basically the growth potential of the economy in terms of labour and capital availability, the stock of skills and available technical progress, and so on. The warranted growth rate is that rate which managers consider justified in terms of their expectation of the income and demand trends in the economy. Applying this to a regional context, it has been seen that both the natural and warranted growth rates in a labour- and capital-inflow region are raised over and above what they otherwise would have been. Management expectations of continued growth are sustained by the availability of the principal factors of production drawn from the L.D.R. Capital and labour shortages are prevented, and the multiplier effect from new investment promotes an acceleration of further demand. This is an extension of Myrdal's 'spread' effect.

The application of Keynesian analysis also shows that trade is less likely to promote self-adjustment or balance between regions than to aggravate initial disparities. The following example again assumes a two-region economy. An autonomous increase in the demand for exports from one region is equivalent to a surplus on its 'current account'. If the import of these goods were paid for by the 'deficit' region through the sale of securities or other means this exchange would 'balance' interregional payments. But as Marina von Neumann Whitman has shown, the crucial question is not the first-round balancing of interregional payments, but the secondary effects in terms of structure and growth in the two regions. The raised profits in the region with expanding exports will attract capital and labour from the import-deficit region. This will be employed both directly in the export sector and in the sectors where income and employment growth are stimulated by the export multiplier. With second-round investment this will tend to result in a divergence between the growth capacity of the two regions, beginning a virtuous circle in the export-led area and a vicious circle in the capital-and labour-outflow region.[9]

Specific factors may offset these cumulative processes. For instance, the L.D.R. may be rich in natural resources. This could mean that it loses capital which otherwise might have been used in transforming its industries, but still gains sufficient payment from primary exports to maintain high income levels in the region. But, in general, the assumption that the free working of the market will aggravate initial interregional disparities is stronger than the self-balance case. One of the most crucial reasons is the difference which most self-balance theory ignores between the responsiveness of labour and capital to differences in interregional earnings. Capital in the form of a savings surplus is almost perfectly responsive to regional differences in the rate of return. It takes only a telephone or a telex call to place it hundreds of miles away. Labour is much less responsive.[10] In practice, sufficient workers may move to the labour-demand region to raise its full-employment ceiling. But this net outflow may be offset by natural population increase in the region of origin, as was the case in the South of Italy, despite massive emigration in the 1950s and 1960s. This will tend to be more likely the greater the initial backwardness of the labour-donor region and the higher the stage of capitalist development of the inflow region, where labour demand in the well-paid manufacturing sector falls off over time with rising capital intensity and the substitution of capital for labour. The demand for labour in services may rise in the M.D.R., and in absolute terms more than offset declining manufacturing employment. But the professional and social skills demanded in many service occupations can act as 'entry barriers' to immigrant labour, leaving them with the dirty or menial service jobs which prove less attractive and exercise less interregional pull.

Historically, this greater loss of capital than labour has been one of the principal causes of the regional problem. In fact the increased dominance of leading firms in national and international markets is now tending to qualify such syphoning of capital from less-developed to more-developed regions. Leading firms tend to rely on retained earnings and fixed interest borrowing (bank overdrafts or bond issues) in order to prevent the loss of managerial control or extension of accountability entailed in continued share issues. Also, many less-developed regions have been so heavily drained over a long period of time that their potential contribution to the finance of growth in more-developed regions has been reduced to relative insignificance. But some theories of regional self-balance still assume that such regions will not lose capital over the long term if labour migration is accelerated. Such arguments are based on the assumption that predominantly rural regions can reduce agricultural under-employment through labour emigration, and thereby raise farm incomes for the remaining labour. Allegedly this will raise income over and above consumption requirements and make capital available for industrial development within the region. This argument frequently falls before it starts because of the higher interregional responsiveness of savings compared with labour flows. It also neglects the barriers to industrial expansion by new firms imposed by already established big-league enterprise. But the argument also fails to take account of the major resource costs of pursuing a policy of accelerated labour migration as a substitute for a policy to develop the problem region through public intervention.

The Costs of Uneven Development

These costs include the age and skill selectivity of emigration to the region of labour outflow. Emigration deprives a less-developed region of its younger and more adaptable labour force, since it is precisely the young and the more enterprising who have the incentive or initiative to move. The process imbalances the age structure of the area and depletes that part of the labour force which in principle would be most attractive to incoming capitalist firms.[11] In this way selectivity in migration further qualifies the assumption in self-balance theory that firms from the M.D.R. will locate plant in the L.D.R. to take advantage of higher labour availability. Some labour migration may be rational in the sense assumed by self-balance theory, but, to the extent that it reduces the most suitable labour for employment training in the region, it aggravates the regional problem. This will result in the under-utilisation of social overhead capital in the region, especially when national governments – on political and social grounds – maintain comparable regional standards through central grants. This can include expenditure on roads and railways, electricity, gas and water supply, public transport services, and housing, health and education.

Inversely, labour inflow to the main centres of production in more-developed regions can result in congestion costs in precisely the same infrastructure. Evidence from the United States, France and Italy shows that the cost of providing new social infrastructure in urban centres with populations greater than 200,000 is higher than in smaller centres, and that such cost differences increase faster the greater the increase in urban population size. These costs are for infrastructure of the same quality.[12] The social or public costs in labour-inflow areas are paralleled by higher private costs in rented or purchased accommodation, transport to and from work, and local taxes or rates.[13] Unless union organisation is low or ineffective, these higher costs will be transferred at least in part to wage demands in firms in the congested region, and thereby increase production costs.

The result of such a situation is a major national imbalance in resource use. Public expenditure in the L.D.R. is not matched by private-enterprise employment, while employment in the M.D.R. means public expenditure at increased cost, and tends to increase wage pressure. The imbalance does not give rise to an automatic interregional self-adjustment. In practice, the interregional imbalance between available labour and actual employment promotes major divergences between private and social costs. These operate not only at the level of social overhead capital but also through the higher wages which firms may have to pay because of the congestion costs borne by labour in the form of higher rent, transport costs and rates in pressured regions. Such costs are in addition to the national income forgone through failure to fully employ the L.D.R. labour force.

Meso-economic Power

These divergences between private and social costs and benefits are only one dimension of the extent to which modern capitalist competition aggravates the regional problem. The self-balance orthodoxy in regional theory has tended to analyse competition between firms in terms of competition for space or competition for markets where firms are price-takers rather than price-makers. In other words, the self-balance analysis has either shunted competition into the cul-de-sac of locational competition, or has stayed in a perfect competition 'never-land' in which markets are composed of firms too small to influence the prices which they can impose on consumers. This has amounted to ignoring the scale economies which firms can secure in production, distribution, servicing, bargaining with suppliers, and access to external finance. It has also meant ignoring the extent to which only large firms are in a position to introduce major innovations and benefit from a high growth of income and demand.

In practice, such scale economies have resulted in what amounts to a dual economic structure in most of the developed capitalist economies. This is not just a dualism between the agricultural and industrial sectors of the economy, but a dualism between different types of industrial firm. According to the micro-economics of orthodox theory, the firm or enterprise generally is too small to dominate particular markets. It responds as 'price-taker' to a sovereign consumer who has choice between a wide range of competing suppliers. When one or a few firms dominate a particular market, the orthodoxy maintains that the consumer still has the chance to import from a lower cost foreign competitor, thereby ensuring price competition, 'normal' profits, and restraining the domination of markets by one or a few firms. But, in fact, the developed capitalist economies are now dominated by a few giant enterprises which exercise what amounts to shared monopoly power in markets. Through restricting consumer choice, they have reversed a dominance of consumer sovereignty into producer sovereignty, in which the big-league firms largely have the power to set prices and lead the market. In some cases their producer power is offset by considerable international competition, for instance in electrical and electronic goods. But in key sectors of these industries such big firms are multi-national in operation, their *own* main competitors in foreign markets, and joint monopolists with other multi-national firms.[14] This increasingly suspends the norm of price competition in international trade to the extent that such firms increase their hold on both national and international markets.

Keynesian economics has been based on synthesis between a micro-economics of firms which are assumed to be price competitive, and a macro-economics of aggregates and over-all policies. But the trend to giant companies has now established a *meso*-economic sector *between* the conventional macro-and micro-economic categories. (Greek *macros* – large; *micros* – small; *mesos* – intermediate.) These are multi-product, multi-company and multi-national enterprises whose size and spread span the gap between micro-and macro-economics. The firms themselves have been variously described as monopolies, oligopolies, leader firms or the 'planning system'. In Marx's analysis of the trend to monopoly, the rise of giant companies was predicted a century ago. In oligopoly analysis, non-Marxist economists have admitted that a few firms can dominate a particular market and behave uncompetitively. François Perroux outlined the role of

pace-setting leader firms (*firmes motrices*) in 1961 and elaborated
the concept in 1965.[15] Galbraith stressed the dominance of big
business in the U.S. economy in the 1960s, and argued that big
firms were forced to 'plan' their markets through a variety of
means which were at variance with the conventional competitive
model of small firms. He maintained that small firms still
abounded, and called them the 'market system'. But the trend to
bigger size meant that these firms were dominated by the giants
in what he called the 'planning system'.[16]

Some theorists of oligopoly have realised the increasingly
central role played by big business in the heartland of the
economy. This is especially true of Bain and Sylos-Labini.[17]
Robert Averitt has identified what we have called meso-
economic firms as 'centre' enterprise, in contrast with 'periphery' firms which conform more closely to the textbook
micro-economic models.[18] By the early 1970s, in both the United
States and Europe, big firms had come to command the centre of
the economic stage and supplant small-scale enterprise as the
dominant mode of production, distribution and exchange.

For instance, in Britain the top 100 companies controlled only
20 per cent of net output in manufacturing in 1950. By 1970
this share had risen to 50 per cent, and on current predictions
will increase to nearly 70 per cent by 1985.[19] In twenty of the
twenty-two main industrial and service sectors in the British
economy, six firms or less control 50 per cent of the assets of the
entire sector.[20] These meso-economic giants are squeezing
thousands of smaller micro-economic firms into the lower third
of their respective industries and services. They corroborate
Marx's prediction a century ago that 'the larger capitals beat the
smaller.... The smaller capitals crowd into spheres of production which modern industry has only sporadically or incomplete-
ly got hold of.'[21] These new meso-economic leaders are notably
multi-national in operation. For instance, in an analysis of 92 of
the top 100 British manufacturing firms between 1950 and
1970, Paul Channon found that those firms with at least six
foreign subsidiaries grew from 23 in 1950 to 30 in 1960, with a
'dramatic increase' to 50 in 1970.[22] And this was a conservative
definition of 'multi-national', since less than six foreign subsidiaries can give a firm access to multi-national location on a major
scale in favoured foreign tax or union havens.

Comparable evidence on a trend to meso-economic domination is available in the other leading capitalist economies. In part, this is no accident since, with the exception of Japan, most of the multi-national companies whose expansion has been so marked through the 1960s have been establishing their meso-economic power through subsidiaries in different countries. The top 100 U.S. manufacturing corporations increased their share of net output from 23 per cent to 33 per cent of the total between 1947 and 1970, and their share of manufacturing assets from nearly 40 per cent to nearly 50 per cent from 1948 to 1971.[23] This share of the meso-economic leaders is highlighted by the fact that in 1970 there were no less than 700,000 active manufacturing corporations in the U.S. economy.[24] Almost certainly, the leaders' rate of domestic market penetration would have been higher had they not been locating more new initiatives abroad than companies in other capitalist countries.[25] Through Western Europe various studies in the early 1970s corroborate the trend to higher concentration of production and assets in the control of leading firms which Bain had noted in the 1960s.[26]

The quantitative distinction between meso-and micro-economic firms is clearly relative. But the quantitative breakdown of meso-economic firms has also to be complemented by a qualitative distinction between their role and that of micro-economic enterprise in the modern capitalist economies. In general, modern capitalism includes both 'leader' firms and 'led' firms. Broadly, the leader firms in investment and product innovation are found in the meso-economic sector. Technical progress in either processes or products may still be pioneered by inspired individuals or small enterprise, but it is mainly the big firms which can afford both to innovate and survive by virtue (or vice) of size.[27] Their lower over-all costs through large-scale and multi-national operation mean that they can secure higher profits and a higher rate of self-financing for any given market price than higher-cost smaller firms.

This has a variety of consequences which are far more consistent with Marx's analysis of monopoly concentration than with the neo-classical mythology of a perfectly competitive market. First, as Bain has shown, such firms can prevent entry into a market by reducing price temporarily to a level which would not enable a high-cost competitor to secure a sufficient return on capital. The larger firms can afford to do this because of initially higher profit levels. They can earn a 'normal' profit while setting a price which would reduce the would-be entrant's profits below those which it can secure in other markets.[28] Secondly, as Sylos-Labini has shown, leading firms can frequently eliminate smaller competitors by reducing price to a level at which the competitor cannot even meet its current costs (such as wage payments). Thirdly, leader firms can employ the threat of such price tactics in order to impose discipline on the smaller 'follower' firms in the particular market. It is this which puts them in a position to lead in the timing, pace and scale of innovations in all save a minority of very exceptional circumstances, whether or not these innovations were based on their own research. Inversely, during periods of either recession or deflation, meso-economic firms can afford to *raise* price to maintain self-financing yet still hold a high proportion of the markets in which they are dominant sellers through size, quality and reliability. Small micro-economic enterprise is less able to do so with impunity, and may go to the wall through cash-flow crises, thereby increasing the trend to monopoly and the rise of meso-economic power.[29]

In practice, this domination of particular markets by meso-economic companies has major regional implications which have been ignored by the exponents of regional self-balance theory. The historical location of such leading firms in national markets has tended to be in the more developed regions and areas. This is not simply an inconvenient coincidence. These regions and areas have become more developed because of the expansion of output and demand by such firms, and the income and employment in ancillary services and distribution developed by them. Many less-developed regions, by the same token, have remained less developed through their lower share of such leading companies. Naturally such a regional dispersion of leading firms in one generation does not mean that the same firms will survive as national leaders for ever. The structural composition of demand also plays an important role. The leading British shipbuilders and coalmine owners of the late nineteenth century produced for most of the world, but have long ago been superseded *via* international competition both for ships and coal, and competition through new forms of transport and power supply.[30] None the less, the trend to meso-economic power in both national and international markets has increased the adaptive capacity of leading firms to structural changes in the pattern of demand. Their super-normal profits in one industry enable them to diversify into others. The spread of operations thereby increases adaptive capacity to demand changes, independently of their power in many cases to influence the pattern of demand through advertising and the creation of consumer wants.

Consequently, smaller firms in less-developed regions are faced with major handicaps in any attempt to penetrate national markets through the exploitation of lower effective wage costs, entrepreneurial skill and government incentives. Such firms may be able to expand their sales to a local market if they produce goods which are marginally different from those served by national leaders. But serious micro-economic confrontation with a meso-leader is likely to result in the leader's retaliation through no-entry pricing, and possibly to the elimination of the smaller firm's profits. In such a circumstance the less-developed region might be better served in the long run if the national leader chooses to take over the plant and facilities producing and employing locally. But if meso-economic firms choose to do this it will be mainly for reasons of labour availability rather than those of labour cost or gains from government regional incentives.[31]

Imbalanced Structure and Location

Meso-economic companies are predominantly multi-national in character. It is mainly the multi-national firm which has sufficient impact on macro-economic aggregates to qualify the micro-economic condition that the firm cannot influence the general level of activity in the national or regional economy. In practice, most of the information on the regional distribution of meso-economic companies takes the form of evidence on foreign multi-national firms. In Britain, France and Italy such analysis dramatically shows the extent to which multi-nationals concentrate their activities in more-developed regions.

For instance, in 1966, half the U.S. multi-nationals in Britain were concentrated in the most-developed South-east of the country, which had only a third of the national population. In the less-developed regions their representation was less than the region's share of national population, with the sole exception of Scotland, where it was within one percentage point of the region's share of total U.K. population.[32]

In France in 1971, the most-developed Paris region represented 19 per cent of national population and 2 per cent of the national surface area. But it included 47 per cent of the plant of foreign multi-national enterprise in the country and 53 per cent of foreign multi-national employment – in other words, some two and a half times the share of the Paris region in national population.[33]

It is argued later that the pull of the metropolitan area on such big-league meso-economic capital is more social than economic. Middle managers, and their wives, want to be near the bright lights of Bond Street or the Champs Elysées, and when multi-nationals frequently oblige such management to do its stint in a less-developed country, they welcome the chance to compensate it by a metropolitan location in more-developed countries.

But even when multi-nationals do locate plant in less-developed regions, they frequently concentrate location in the more-developed part of the L.D.R., rather than in the more peripheral locations where jobs in modern manufacturing may be most needed to secure a balanced job mix. Thus in Italy in the early 1970s, after some twenty-five years of regional development policy, 70 per cent of both manufacturing plant and jobs located in the Mezzogiorno by foreign multi-national companies was concentrated in the more-developed Lazio and Campania regions.[34]

Disaggregation by sector of the regional penetration of foreign multi-national capital in France, Italy and Britain shows a marked concentration in modern rather than traditional industries.

For instance, the DATAR study on foreign capital in France shows that there is a strong representation in the dynamic and faster growing modern industries such as precision machinery, electrical machinery and appliances, electronics, chemicals and chemical products, non-ferrous metals, agricultural machinery and equipment, rubber and plastics as well as oil and petrol. It draws attention to the fact that such companies tend to be vertically integrated on a multi-national scale, with plant in less-developed countries. It stresses that the productivity and returns to such multi-nationals in modern industry are in general considerably higher than for industry as a whole. But it also emphasises the unequal rate of penetration which derives from their 'privileged position based on other reasons (than sectoral composition) including principally their size of operation, their operation in several countries, and their innovation in both products and techniques'. Significantly, in view of our distinction of meso-and micro-economic enterprise, the report observes that, in productivity terms, foreign multi-nationals have no effective rivals except very large French firms.[35]

In Italy, similarly, foreign multi-national capital in the Mezzogiorno is concentrated in petroleum, chemicals, plastics, pharmaceuticals, non-metallic minerals, rubber, electrical engineering, electronics and food processing. Benetti, Ferrara and Medori not only show the concentration of such foreign investment in the more-developed part of the South, but also stress the extent to which foreign capital pre-empts national or regional control over the more advanced industrial sectors which, precisely because they are more advanced, are critical for effective regional development. They admit that in certain sectors the penetration of foreign multi-national capital is effectively blocked by major national enterprise in either the private or the public sector (for example the state holding companies). But they illustrate the difficulties for regional policy makers in the event of foreign multi-nationals deciding to close down operations, either through reaction to increased trade-union pressure on wages and working conditions, or as a reaction to recession in trade. In some cases, multi-nationals have withdrawn from the South of Italy after having benefited from regional development aid on their investment, and shift location to other European regions or the Third World, where they can gain further state aid for the new location.[36]

The most detailed analysis of the question of multi-national dependence and control in the British economy has been undertaken by John Firn in relation to Scotland. Firn stresses that Scotland appears exceptional in its high degree of dependence on externally controlled enterprise. He defines external control in such a way as to include companies whose ownership and ultimate decision-making levels are outside Scotland. His findings very much corroborate our previous analysis of the domination of meso-economic, multi-national capital over micro-economic enterprise, and its concentration (as in France and Italy) in the more modern, dynamic sectors critical to effective regional development.

Thus Firn found that (i) only 41 per cent of Scottish manufacturing employment was controlled internally, (ii) that the larger the enterprise, the greater the likelihood that it was controlled externally, (iii) that over a quarter of total manufacturing employment was in branch plants of externally controlled enterprise, (iv) that nearly 46 per cent of total employment was accounted for by 110 enterprises each employing more than 1000 people, (v) that the faster growing the sector the lower the share of Scottish participation, and (vi) that the five fastest growing sectors – including chemicals and allied industries, electrical engineering and vehicles – had less than 14 per cent indigenous control. He illustrates what we have called the dualism between meso-and micro-economic enterprise by the fact that small-scale local entrepreneurs, being excluded from the faster growing modern industries, are setting up enterprise in the Clydeside conurbation in what are actually declining sectors of the economy.

Firn also emphasises that the high degree of dependence of employment in modern manufacturing industry on external control 'would make it almost impossible for an independent Scottish government to run an independent economic policy... and implies that (external) economic fluctuations are transmitted to the Scottish economy fairly quickly'. As he adds, 'this situation is also harder to identify, let alone control, as international trade increasingly becomes a matter not just of trade between large multinational companies, but of trade between the different operating units *within* multinational enterprises'.[37]

Multi-nationals versus the Regions

Such questions of external dependence and control clearly have major implications for the question of regional devolution. An independent Scotland might well find itself limited to physical land-use planning rather than effective economic planning in any meaningful sense. It also could find itself forced to resort to tax concessions in the hope of attracting foreign multi-national capital rather than effective taxation of big business in the main growth sectors of the economy.

This is particularly likely granted the difficulties which larger nation states such as Britain are experiencing in the control of multi-national company location. In general, there has been a discernable trend since the later 1960s towards multi-national rather than multi-regional location by leading meso-economic enterprise. The basic reason is the fact that in relatively labour-intensive production leading national firms now can secure far larger gains by going multi-national than by going multi-regional. These gains are focused in three main areas: labour costs, tax avoidance, and leverage on national governments. For instance, multi-national companies' labour costs in Third World countries are as little as 10 to 25 per cent the cost of labour in the United Kingdom. By transfer pricing, or the arranging of prices in transactions between their multi-national subsidiaries, these companies can also ensure that tax is minimised or avoided in high tax capitalist economies and syphoned to Switzerland or other tax havens. Also, as the same evidence confirms, as well as from the experience of regional development officials, such companies can employ the threat (either veiled or blunt) of a location of new plant abroad in order to exercise leverage on governments to allow them to expand outside problem regions in the 'host' country.[38]

The division of a production sequence in different world-wide plant undermines the conventional wisdom that firms will choose to locate near firms in related activities, or near final markets, in order to secure external economies of location. It also qualifies the assumption that transport costs rise significantly with distance, causing firms to agglomerate in 'polarised' centres of activity. The Perroux polarisation thesis and the popularity of the 'polarisation' orthodoxy has tended in practice to provide leading world companies with a rationale which cloaks the real nature of their global location policy. This is partly because of the spurious realism of the polarisation concept, which is expressed as dynamic imbalance rather than the static self-balance of the neo-classical regional theorists. Also, available evidence indicates that some firms *do* need to locate near suppliers and markets if they are to survive. But these tend to be small companies producing for rapidly changing markets, or small firms whose survival in modern industry has been mainly through holding the coat tails of faster-moving and better-managed enterprises to which they act as suppliers or sub-contractors. The meso-economic leaders divide their own production multi-nationally, and globally internalise many of the economies which smaller enterprise would externalise to local firms.[39]

The plain fact is that national economies no longer are 'isolated states' of the kind originally hypothesised in location analysis by von Thünen.[40] Freedom to export capital into productive enterprise abroad not only has undermined the basis of orthodox neo-classical trade theory, but has also undermined the assumption that 'pressured' firms in more-developed regions must seek more or cheaper labour in less-developed regions in the same country. As already indicated, multi-national operation gives leading meso-economic companies access to labour in less-developed countries at a fraction of the cost of labour in problem areas in developed economies. For instance, the Financial Director of the Burroughs Company in Britain submitted to the Commons Expenditure Committee that 'along with all other companies [it] is locating in Taiwan, Brazil, Mexico, the Philippines and Hong Kong, where the cost of labour is very, very low'. When asked how low, he replied that it was about one-quarter of the cost of labour in a British Development Area (problem region). Evidence from the U.S. Tariff Commission and other sources show that in fact Far East and Mexican labour costs range from one-tenth to as little as one-twentieth of U.S. labour costs, depending on area and product.[41]

This phenomenon of location in less developed countries rather than less-developed regions might be more attractive if the multi-nationals thereby clearly benefited the Third World.

But, in practice, the benefits from multi-national location to host countries in the Third World are limited. They amount mainly to direct employment and wage creation. The external spread effect from such companies is negligible precisely because they internalise so much of their production sequence in different less-developed countries before importing the product either complete or at the final stage of assembly and packaging to developed-country markets. This means that there is little or no spread effect by the multi-national in building up local growth centres or ancillary supplier industries. Also, less developed countries have started a competitive upwards bidding in concessions to multi-national enterprise. This includes up to fifteen-year 'tax holidays', or no tax revenue for local public expenditure or social-welfare benefits. It also includes union holidays, or the guarantee that unions will not disrupt smooth and continuous production essential to an enterprise whose global whole is so dependent on its constituent parts. In practice this means either no unions, or unionists tamed by unfriendly night visitors.[42]

Further, from a regional viewpoint, there is a considerable aggravation of urban–rural dualism to the extent that multi-national manufacturing enterprise tends to locate in premier central-area sites, and frequently the suburbs of the main metropolitan area itself. Some multi-national companies specialise in tailoring their production to local skills and requirements, but normally under contract from the local government (Booker McConnell is a good example). Very few multi-nationals co-operate extensively with the regional development priorities of less-developed countries, or assist with the establishment of sub-metropolitan growth centres. None of this should be surprising when multi-nationals have sufficient blackmail power through alternative international locations to impose tax-haven conditions on the government of Eire (the Shannon free zone) and to successfully resist British government pressure to locate in problem regions when it does not suit their immediate interests.[43]

The trend to multi-national versus multi-regional location is qualified by some political factors. For one thing, the mature capitalist economies in general have been considered safer politically by multi-national management. In other words, their governments have hitherto been considered less likely to nationalise the multi-national's subsidiaries than those in some less-developed countries which have come to power on a wave of nationalist reaction against foreign exploitation. In practice this tends to mean that relatively capital-intensive investment is located in Western Europe by U.S. multi-nationals, with the further contributory factor that European countries offer a higher initial complement of skills and inputs than are available in less-developed countries.

None the less, the trend to location in those less-developed countries which exhibit decidedly non-socialist tendencies has been accelerating rapidly since the mid-1960s. Burroughs is not alone in its choice of host countries. As Henry Ford II has said, 'in South Korea, Taiwan, and Indonesia we see promising markets and an attractive supply of cheap labour'.[44] From 1966 the U.S. television, camera and clothing industries were joining electronics and automobiles in a flight to certain countries in the Third World which has rightly given rise to the label of 'runaway industries'. By the 1970s, George Meany cited a Congressional estimate that 20 per cent of cars, 40 per cent of glassware, 60 per cent of sewing machines and calculators, *all* casettes and radios, and large proportions of clothing manufacture had already been displaced by imports, a large proportion of which was coming from U.S.-owned foreign factories. But the trend is not limited to manufactures. It also hits agriculture in less-developed regions as the 'agri-business' multi-nationals extend their range. Thus, as Barnet and Müller cite, 'American food-processing companies now export frozen Mexican strawberries in great quantities to the United States, forcing the Louisiana strawberry industry to shift nearly half the acreage planted in strawberries to other uses'. They add that 'today labour statesmen are vocal in denouncing the "runaway shop" yet understandably confused as to what to do about it'.[45]

In the late 1960s two U.S. food multi-nationals started moves to take over three leading Italian food companies. When asked by the government to what extent they intended to use and process southern produce, and what proportion of their new investment they would locate in the South, they replied that they intended to import from Israel and locate expansion in North Italy. In this case the Italian government knew what action to take. In the interest of Italian labour in the South they brought the three threatened companies into public ownership through the State Holding company, I.R.I., and obliged I.R.I. to draw up plans for the expansion of all their new plant in the South of Italy, using southern produce as much as possible for food processing, and integrating sales of the products into the I.R.I. supermarket retail chains.[46]

Thereby, of course, hangs a moral which may not be lost in future to Mr Meany and the American labour movement. Its pressures on the U.S. government in favour of job protection in the United States would be welcome to the extent that it insisted on the location of a high share of new public enterprises in U.S. problem regions, and argued the case for government support in making U.S. multi-nationals in the Third World more accountable for tax, more ready to integrate production with local firms in regional growth centres, and more responsive to union rights.

CHAPTER 3

THE LIMITS OF LIBERAL CAPITALIST POLICIES

Most regional development policies to date have been undertaken in what can be described as a liberal capitalist framework. Thus the policies have largely been attempted in a framework of *in*direct intervention in favour of problem regions and areas. This operates through attempts to persuade companies to locate in problem regions by the offering of incentives rather than direct intervention to ensure particular locations. The incentives take two main forms: (1) cash aids and allowances available to the firms; and (2) improvement of infrastructure and the offering of on-site facilities in problem areas. In a few countries such 'positive' incentives to firms have been supplemented by 'negative' incentives or disincentives. These can take the form of congestion taxes and levies on location outside problem areas and regions, and in Britain have included the use of Industrial Development Certificates as a disincentive to expansion in developed regions.

The Gelding of Aids and Incentives

The rationale of regional aids and incentives is rarely made explicit. Much of the theory of regional development is elaborated in a policy vacuum, and government policy statements in many cases are made without reference to an economic rationale or justification. One of the main reasons has been the extent to which the theory has assumed that – at least over the long run – price competitive, cost-minimising firms would seek those locations which gave them the greatest operating advantage, including location in national regions with the highest labour availability and lowest labour cost. By the same token, government policies which have increased existing aids or introduced new ones have assumed a basically price competitive framework in the capitalist economy,

The trend to meso-economic power and multi-national capital has substantially undermined this assumed price competitive framework for precisely those firms whose over-all size, market position, professional management and multi-plant structure makes them most suited as instruments of regional development. In other words, indirect incentives and disincentives no longer bite effectively on the leader firms in manufacturing and some modern services whose geographical mobility has been demonstrated by their world-wide location of plant and offices.

Basically, the rationale of incentives assumes that firms either need or can use low-cost or free money on the scale offered by the government. Similarly, the rationale of disincentives assumes that firms are penalised in cost terms by congestion levies or by the refusal of permission to expand production or operations outside national problem regions. But the 'pull' rationale of incentives overlooks the extent to which leading firms in the meso-economic sector can secure greater gains through domestic market domination and multi-national location than most regional incentives can offer them. Similarly, the 'push' rationale of disincentives overlooks the ability of a multi-national company to put its new plant abroad if not permitted to locate in a developed area.

Bluntly, the pull effect of incentives depends on firms being price-takers rather than price-makers. It assumes a world of consumer sovereignty in which substitution between alternative suppliers acts as an incentive to companies to keep profits closely aligned with costs and seek only a 'normal' rate of profit. In practice, however, the era of producer sovereignty has already been with us for a long time. It arose essentially through the phenomenon which most regional self-balance theory ignores – economies of scale in production, purchasing, management, distribution and access to finance. Such producer sovereignty gives meso-economic firms the power to impose prices higher than increases in costs. Yet if such firms can increase their net profits through an x per cent price increase, they will hardly be attracted to a less developed region by an equivalent x per cent incentive. After all, why should they trouble to organise an entirely new regional venture when they could make the same cash gain by staying put and raising prices? Under the kind of inflation experienced from the mid-1960s to the mid-1970s, such price-making power would have been likely to have a considerable erosion effect on incentives.

In general it is clear that lower costs from size allow productivity gains in the meso-economic sector which are not transmitted in full to lower prices. In many cases, oil crises and exceptional commodity price rises apart, leading companies in national markets will need to dispose of their profit surplus abroad or see it eroded by both government taxation and union wage pressure if it is fully declared. The result is the syphoning of profits through the transfer-pricing mechanism to numbered bank accounts and tax havens abroad, frequently into the multi-national companies' own banking subsidiary. The ironies of this erosion of the pull effect of regional incentives in liberal capitalist States are very clear. It is not so much that leading national companies can afford to ignore major regional incentives, but that they cannot afford to accept them. The reason lies in the new dimension to the 'follow-the-leader' mechanism which is supposed to underlie the competitive process. In such a competitive model a new entrant to a market is supposed to be able to reduce any monopoly profits by pricing products nearer to cost than the monopolists. As a result the monopolist will have to follow his lead or lose his market share. Under conditions of multi-national competition, even a leading national company whose board is concerned to act in the interest of problem regions and areas cannot afford to accept the lower profits which regional incentives offer relative to the labour cost and transfer-pricing gains offered by a multi-national location.

Evidence from both British and U.S. multi-national companies shows that the scale of regional incentives which they discount in Britain has been staggering. Such incentives have included grants ranging up to 40 per cent of investment costs, and subsidies on labour costs (Regional Employment Premiums). Unilever submitted to the House of Commons Expenditure Committee that it was 'unable to produce evidence from our own experience that the Regional Employment Premium has increased investment or employment in the Development Areas'. Cadbury Schweppes submitted that neither labour nor capital incentives played a major role in location decisions. G.K.N. stated that 'the attraction of the incentives has so far been inadequate'. Tube Investments said that 'there are not many projects where regional policy is of critical importance to the strategic decision (to locate)'.[1]

These meso-economic multi-national companies are not acting irrationally in such discounting. The fact is that labour costs in less-developed countries can give them a 75 per cent gain on costs in British problem regions, while transfer pricing can permit tax avoidance for profits on particular products ranging from more than the gain from investment grants to several hundred per cent. The precise scale of such syphoned profits is not known, though an indication was given in 1973 by the case between the British Monopolies Commission and the Swiss-based pharmaceuticals company Hoffman La Roche. A further indication of the undermining of the 'pull' effect of incentives and the 'push' effect of location controls was given to the Commons Expenditure Committee by the I.B.M. company. I.B.M. admitted that it informed the British government that it would locate a new plant abroad if it were not allowed to locate it in an already developed area in the South of England, where it would have secured no regional aids. I.B.M. won this unequal contest, and gained the developed area location of its choice – at Havant.[2]   Clearly not all manufacturing or modern services companies are equally able to ignore regional incentives and disincentives. Leading meso-economic firms are followed not only by those firms which they lead, but also lagging companies which trail at the lower-quality and profit end of the market. Meso-economic firms in manufacturing and head-office national services such as banking and insurance are essential to the transformation of national problem regions because they are the most mobile firms in the most mobile sectors of the economy. When they have either inherited a plant or office in a problem region through taking over a previous company located there, or have decided on such a location for reasons independent of government aid (such as labour availability or good trout fishing), they still receive the full range of government financial assistance as of right. In practice, of course, their dominant national and multi-national position means that the failure to discriminate between them and smaller local firms further handicaps the latter in any possible challenge to the leaders' dominance, The scale of the cost and profit differentials is already so vast that the best hope for regional laggards now lies partly in the abolition of regional aid for specified categories of leader firms, and partly in sub-contracting so as to take on the role of satellite supplier. In the latter case either the central government or a regional planning agency may have to play broker to the contract if it actually is to occur.

The Limits of Improving Infrastructure

The other main arm of indirect or liberal capitalist regional policies is the provision of infrastructure and the local concentration of development programmes in growth centres or poles. The role of infrastructure can be clarified by the distinction between social overhead capital (S.O.C.) and economic overhead capital (E.O.C.). The evidence demonstrates that private company management is only concerned with a limited category of general social overhead capital. This is, essentially, good housing, education, recreation and health facilities for itself and its 'imported' skilled personnel. Economic overhead capital includes sufficient site area for expansion, the provision of power and water supply, telecommunications and transport access, and accommodation for plant, warehousing, and so on.

The difficulties of attracting firms to problem areas and regions through the provision of such S.O.C. and E.O.C. facilities are obvious enough, but very frequently neglected by those theorists and policy-makers trapped within the framework of the conventional competitive model. For instance, it has been widely assumed that the provision of more space for on-site expansion in a Development Area or Growth Centre will attract a firm which finds its quarters cramped in a 'congested area'. But this ignores factors which reduce the pull effect of having room to expand. The first is the already summarised counter-pull of a location abroad. The second is the counter-weight which a leading national or multi-national company can exercise on the central government even if the latter is operating a disincentives policy for developed areas in the form of a congestion tax or location controls. This can include the frequently forceful claim that location of new capacity and jobs several hundred miles from already established centres will divert management resources from other aspects of company activity such as contributing to the national 'export drive'. The force lies more in the government's short-term concern with such dimensions of national policy than any long-term merits of the argument, especially if 'over-development' outside high-unemployment regions is already contributing to a cost-push inflation which underlies the need for export drives in the first place. (It should be noted that the coincidence of cost-push inflation and the syphoning of super-normal profits is not in any sense contradictory. Some of the 'led' and most of the 'laggard' manufacturers will feel real cost-push pressures through effective union wage bargaining, while the declared profits of the leader firms will be lower than real profits because of transfer pricing. The resultant inflationary pressures therefore will be real enough for smaller firms, while absorbed with relative ease by the larger.)

A further important reason for a low pull effect from the provision of adequate infrastructure lies in the distinction between social overhead capital and economic overhead capital. It is not difficult for governments to ensure that E.O.C. of adequate specification and quality is provided in problem regions, at least in the more developed and administratively more efficient economies. But the provision of such infrastructure is a *necessary* rather than a *sufficient* condition for regional development. Leading companies will not flock to less-developed regions simply because E.O.C. in terms of on-site facilities is as good as E.O.C. they can secure in the developed areas. Also, the cost saving from low-rent sites and facilities will not be significant for a leading multi-national company. More importantly, less-developed regions can rarely hope to compete with the S.O.C. facilities of developed regions, and in particular those served by a major metropolitan centre. One of the most important facilities of such centres is the frequency of international air flights from nearby airports. Added to this is the concentration of quality private housing, private education and private health facilities for busy executives. Besides which, only the major centres can provide a wide range of entertainment for the professional management grades, including cinema and theatre, restaurants, clubs, and so on. And this is apart from the role of major centres in providing job opportunities for the

manager's wife, frequently a graduate with professional training, whether or not she is also a member of women's lib.[3] Even
the unliberated woman will exercise influence on her husband
to press for a job location less than a hundred miles from major
stores and fashion centres.

In other words, to rely on a policy of improving social
infrastructure in problem regions is a Sisyphus fate. By
definition the areas which need to attract management most will
be those least attractive to them. Governments and local
authorities may push indefinitely to improve the general
attractiveness of a particular area, and thereby serve the indirect
function of improving it for local inhabitants, which is no mean
achievement. But a slum-free corridor between a middle-class
housing estate and a new industrial site will be no competition
for the total social pull of the downtown areas of Milan,
Hamburg, Paris or London.

Mistakes in Growth-Centre Policy

The growth-centre or growth-pole policy is favoured by many
governments in Western Europe, and is now coming into
fashion in the United States. The intellectual and economic
foundations of this policy range from slim to false. The false
premise is the claim that firms need to locate near each other in
order to secure technological external economies, and to gain
from the proximity of other firms in related industries. This was
clearly true in the early stages of capitalist development, when
the high costs of transport and the specialisation of firms in a
production process split between different companies gave
advantages from a close location of related stages in that process.
But the growth of large-scale companies has substantially been
through the internalisation of such different stages of production in one company. Besides which, transport costs in manufacturing have now been reduced below the minimum addition to
total costs likely to be agreed in many union wage agreements.
Net distance costs are so insigificant that very few firms even
keep a systematic account of them. Again, this can be seen most
clearly in the case of the multi-national leaders who now account
for the bulk of manufacturing output in the developed
capitalist economies. These companies largely internalise the

successive stages of their own products and spread their plant to at least three of the four corners of the world.

As with the case for incentives in general, there are differences in the importance of proximity for different types of firm. This most clearly emerges, however, in small firms with a limited range of final or component products, especially in markets with rapidly changing specifications and tastes. These now account for a minor share of output in the mobile manufacturing sector, and small firms in the services sector tend to be tied, by definition, to specific locations (for example retailing and personal services). In many cases such small micro-economic firms may cluster around meso-economic leaders in spatially concentrated complexes. But they do so less for external-economy benefits which such locations offer than because the leader firm has built them up on an original location as a satellite contractor or supplier of goods and services. They survive not by virtue of the collective strength secured from a shared production process with equally small firms, but because of the grace and favour of the larger firms already there which can use them. The replacement investment alone of the leader firms will tend to ensure that such complexes grow once they have been established. But this is the result of internal expansion through internal economies rather than the proximity gains from external economics as hypothesised in the growth-centre literature.

For such reasons no government can expect to secure success in the development of a problem region through the establishment of growth poles or centres unless it requires a leading firm or firms to locate major plant there and build up satellite supplier linkages. So far very few governments operating in the framework of liberal capitalist policies have identified this imperative, far less taken means to implement it. The reason is partly the mesmeric hold of the competitive market myth and the assumption that companies will be attracted to designated growth centres in problem regions by a combination of incentives and disincentives. It is on such assumptions that the French and Italian governments, for example, have offered higher regional aids and concessions in scheduled growth areas and centres than are available elsewhere in their problem regions. The differential is considerable, with nearly double the

incentives available in the special centres.[5] But the pull effect
fails in its effect on the large multi-plant firms which is essential
to the success of the policy. The policy arm is fractured by the
alternative gains available to these firms from dominant
positions in national markets and the attraction of locations in
less-developed countries and tax havens. Doubling the incentives therefore has next to no effect.

The Failure of Indicative Regional Planning

Indicative regional planning became the white hope of frust-
rated regional departments in the early 1960s. In France it took
the form of new statements of intention to 'regionalise' the
national planning process – a process which had already become
the model for introducing 'coherence' in liberal capitalist policy
abroad. In Italy, indicative planning for the regions was the key
priority behind the study programmes and econometric exercises which preceded the introduction of the 1966 National Plan.
In Britain, the model of French indicative planning was
imported as the basis of the 1965 National Plan, and was
advertised as a powerful new instrument for the transformation
of national and regional growth.

By the early 1970s the white hope had proved yet another
white elephant. The degree of disillusionment varied with the
degree of failure and disenchantment. In Britain, the National
Plan was aborted soon after take-off by the wide-reaching
deflationary measures of July 1966. Regional Economic Planning Councils were maintained in being, but since the National
Plan had been suspended they were left to find their own future
role and function. Without economic targets translated down
from the national level, this amounted to the drawing of physical
land-use and environment plans for the newly scheduled
planning regions. These looked handsome on paper, but the
Planning Councils had no independent powers of any signifi-
cance and they remained indicative in a purely figurative sense.

In France, regionalisation of the National Plan was quickly
appreciated as the fig leaf masking a policy of national economic
expansion based as before on the dominance of the Paris region.
Parliamentary pressure in a debate of November 1963 resulted
in the publication a year later of a forecasting exercise which

projected the regional structure of the national economy to 1985. But this only forecasted present trends (rather than outlined means to change them), and merely broke down national data into three main regions.[6] Instruments to implement a new policy to counterbalance the attraction of Paris were introduced in the form of newly scheduled growth centres, designed to reinforce fines for expanding in the Paris area without permission for certain categories of firms. In 1964 a new regional office was established which was directly responsible to the Prime Minister, and from the same year the national budget carried an annex which spelled out the scheduled national government expenditure by region.[7] But these new institutions were not effectively linked or coordinated in a national planning framework designed to secure a decisive change in the French regional imbalance. The incentives in the *métropoles* did not bite with any depth; the fines in Paris were too low or were ignored by government departments themselves; the regionalised budget articulated what would in any event have been the case, and the Prime Minister's new office operated more as a means of mediating conflict between interest groups than transforming the nature of the problem. That problem was aggravated in terms of the disparity between Paris and the rest of the country increasing over the years 1962–9, and in 1971 the Prime Minister's office published another forecasting exercise for French regions for the year 2000 which bore the ominously likely sub-title: *Scenario of the Unacceptable.*[8]

In Italy a ten-year national development programme published in December 1954, and known popularly as the Vanoni Plan, identified the development of the problem region of the South as one of three main national priorities (together with national full employment and balance-of-payments equilibrium). It also identified what it called 'propulsive sectors' whose expansion would be guaranteed through local authorities, financed through funds in the State Development Bank for the South (*Cassa per il Mezzogiorno*). This was supplemented in 1957 by the designation of new growth areas and nuclei, comparable with the Perroux growth pole, which would carry higher incentives and aids to location than available elsewhere in the South. But, in practice, the alleged 'propulsive sectors' of the Vanoni Plan were the infrastructural sectors of power, water

supply, and road improvement, rather than modern manufacturing, and the expenditure of the Development Bank for the
South tended to substitute for what the local authorities and
national   government   otherwise   would   have   spent   on
infrastructure.[9]

A major series of parliamentary debates in January and
February 1961 sustained eight motions from both the main
parties of the left and the left wing of the Christian Democratic
Party which criticised the government's failure to make a reality
of the planning targets of the Vanoni Plan, and urged the
introduction of more effective planning instruments. A committee under Professor Ugo Papi spent a year in the elaboration
of a highly Anglo-Saxon draft programme, based explicitly on
Harrod–Domar capacity assumptions, and projecting three
alternative growth paths which the government might 'indicate'
to national and regional enterprise for the 1962–70 period. The
document raised a major parliamentary outcry since it only
published a statement of the need for more effective regional
policy, rather than the means to achieve it, and even failed to
make a regional breakdown of its main national projections. A
new National Commission for Economic Planning was established, followed by a further and more specifically regionalised
draft programme, drawn up under the chairmanship of the
main author of the Vanoni Plan, Professor Pasquale Saraceno.
By 1965 this had been followed by the publication of a new
indicative planning document, the Giolitti Plan, which set targets
for both government expenditure and employment in the
South, scheduled a reorientation of the Development Bank for
the South towards industrial initiatives, recommended penalties
for expansion in the 'congested' areas of the North, and also
proposed 'regulation of the location decisions of large scale
enterprise'.[10] But the government of which Giolitti was the
Budget Minister fell the day before his document could have
become law. His successor, Giovanni Pieraccini, drew up a
weaker revised document intended to cover the period 1966–70
which dropped the references to measures on congestion
penalties and regulation of the location decisions of large-scale
enterprise. This document only gained parliamentary approval
in July 1967 – more than six years after the first parliamentary
pressure for advance on the Vanoni Plan, and half way through

the 1965–9 period which the Giolitti Plan was intended to cover.[11]

In practice, it would have been disastrous for the Italian national economy if leading private enterprise had waited for parliamentary approval of such an indicative plan before proceeding with its own production and location decisions. As it was, it largely did what it had decided to do on its own private cost–benefit grounds, with the result that the share of the South in national manufacturing employment fell over the 1951–67 period. The situation would have been worse if the government had waited for the elaboration and passage through parliament of an indicative plan before obliging its public enterprises in 1957 to locate specified proportions of total investment and investment in entirely new plant in the South. It was this investment which prevented a worse decline in the share of the South in manufacturing employment, and actually improved the South's share in those manufacturing sectors in which public enterprise was substantially represented.[12]

Four general conclusions can be drawn from the experience of indicative regional planning in these three countries.

First, an indicative planning framework will not persuade leading capitalist firms to do what they choose not to do. Classically, the French indicative plans in the 1950s were supposed to overcome the information problem for firms faced with risk and uncertainty in a competitive market. The government's statement of good intentions for the various sectors of the economy was therefore supposed to substitute for the 'perfect knowledge' of perfect competition textbooks. But firms which had established an effectively dominant market position by the 1960s had little or no need of information on government intentions except in either a very broad sense, or from meetings with economic ministers and officials.

Secondly, the incorporation of regional incentives and aids in an indicative planning document does not transform the low pull effect of such policies for leading firms whose dominant market share or multi-national alternatives offer cash gains far in excess of what the government can offer. Incorporating such incentives in a statement of indicative targets wraps an already empty box with statistical trimmings.

Thirdly, the spinning of these trimmings in the relevant

government departments, or independent agencies, can become an obstacle to the introduction of more direct and effective regional policy instruments. This is partly a matter of time, whether the elaboration is on handloom jennies or new-generation computers. The year's delay in the preparation of an Italian indicative plan, through the rejection of the Papi Report, has already been mentioned. In the British case the story is longer and worse. In 1965 the British planning ministry (Department of Economic Affairs) invited the independent National Institute of Economic and Social Research 'to build up a theoretical and empirical framework for the analysis of regional economic development and the consideration of regional policy in the United Kingdom, especially in relation to problems of national economic development'. A substantial grant was made and the Institute's report was published *seven years later* in 1972.[13] By then two general elections had occurred and the Labour Government which initiated the study had been out of power for two years – substantially through failure of its own traditional supporters in problem regions and areas to vote for it at the polls.

Fourthly, even rapidly devised indicative plans for problem regions have not been able to establish regional development as a national priority. This is partly an economic matter and partly a matter of contradictions in policies. One of the most important has been the conflict between international and regional economic policy. In both Italy and France leading national companies through the late 1950s and early 1960s were able to maintain to the national planners that they could either reinforce their competitive strength in the E.E.C. or locate new initiatives in problem regions, but not both. Thus the emerging conflict of multi-national versus multi-regional companies in recent years has been paralleled by an increasing conflict for governments between international integration and regional disintegration.

CHAPTER 4

THE REGION IN INTERNATIONAL INTEGRATION

In the early 1970s one of the most central issues in the policy debate on the E.E.C. is whether higher stages of integration will aggravate rather than reduce the regional problem. In fact there are two main dimensions to the issue: (1) the problem of national regions and national regional policies in a Community framework; and (2) the problems and prospects for nations themselves as regions in a single-currency area of the kind which would be created if the Community is successful in implementing its monetary-union proposals. There also now is the question in reverse: i.e. the issue whether a country-region such as Scotland has suffered from integration into the single currency area of the United Kingdom, and should not pressure for economic and monetary disintegration, 'going it alone' as a nation-region with autonomous powers. The French government in the early 1970s also was formally committed to monetary union in the E.E.C., without accepting that this should be accompanied by economic union of major national policies administered by a supra-national or federal authority. None the less, the two main cases of international economic integration in modern capitalist economies concern pre-federal and federal systems – the E.E.C. and the U.S. federal economy – and their examination in the light of regional and integration theory respectively can illuminate the kind of regional problem thrown up by international integration.

One of the remarkable aspects of the current programme for monetary integration in the E.E.C. is the fact that, although it has been urged by pressure groups such as the powerful Action Committee for a United States of Europe, very little specific attention has been paid to the impact of the U.S. federal system on regional structure and the spatial allocation of resources in a single-currency area. Much attention has been given to the favourable stimulus to economic growth assumed to have followed from the large domestic market of the United States. Jean Monnet, according to Fourastié and Courthéoux, was impressed by the capacity of the Americans to mobilise a war economy in the early 1940s virtually without reduction of civilian peacetime consumption levels.[1]

More recently, and sensationally, Jean-Jacques Servan-Schreiber entertained a wide audience with his analysis of the American challenge to Europe through the penetration of the E.E.C. economy by U.S. multi-nationals, and recommended that the European response be found in the development of an E.E.C. economy which was sufficiently integrated to provide European companies with the size of market and the economies of scale which could enable them to compete on an equal footing at home with U.S. companies.[2] But little attention has been paid to the historical differences between the gradual integration of the U.S. economy in the nineteenth and early twentieth centuries, and the question of integrating already developed economies under different domestic and international conditions. In particular, and perhaps not surprisingly granted the failure of the U.S. government until the 1960s to take account of the scale of its own regional problems, it appears to have been assumed, either that the United States had no regional problem outside the Deep South (whose problems were mainly considered racial–political), or that they were of a lesser order than in Europe, due to the automatic reduction of regional disparities with higher stages of economic growth.[3] Chapter 5 analyses the E.E.C. regional problem in both the pre-federal and pre-monetary integration periods. Chapter 6 evaluates features of the regional problem in the U.S. federal economy, with an attempt to indicate the lessons which might be learned in advance for the regional gains and losses from a single-currency or federal system. To clarify some of the main issues both chapters also link some of the common elements in regional theory and in the theory of international economic integration.

Integration Economics and Regional Theory

It could reasonably be claimed that the economics of international integration is regional economics writ large. The parallelism between regional theory and international integration theory is clear enough. Both tend to concern geographically contiguous areas; both concern not only trade but also the movement of labour and capital; both show a conflict between self-balance and imbalance theory. On the other hand, regional theory within nation states mainly concerns the explanation of the mechanism of spatial distribution of resources in a single-currency economy with a single central government, a homogeneous capital market and institutions, a national system of company law and taxation, and a labour force at least nominally united in terms of language. By contrast, the theory of economic integration concerns the process of inter-penetration of economies with initially different governments, currencies, capital markets and institutions, company legislation, taxation, and language. Regional economics may raise the question whether one should originally have integrated at all (for example Italy in 1861) rather than maintained different economies with separate governments, currencies, and so on. But it is basically concerned with already integrated systems, at least in a nominal or formal sense (since national regions may, in practice, be disintegrated through 'backwash' effects from leading regions). By contrast, integration economics raises the issue whether to integrate in the first place, and if so how far the process of integration should proceed.

The distinction can be clarified by spelling out five main stages of integration which fall between the extremes of an independent national economy, and a national economy which has become so highly integrated with another or other economies as to constitute a sub-region of them (such as Scotland or Wales in the United Kingdom). These include (1) a free trade area, in which internal tariffs between countries have been abolished, but their previous tariffs towards other countries maintained; (2) a customs union, where a common tariff is established for imports from third countries in addition to the internal abolition of tariffs towards other members of the union; (3) a common market, which might be thought an appropriate term for either a free-trade area or a customs union, but in practice tends to be applied to a customs union which also proceeds with the liberalisation of labour and capital flows; (4) an economic union, in which some national policies are harmonised in spheres other than trade policy or labour and capital movements, with responsibility for their enforcement remaining with the member states; and (5) economic federalism, in which certain policies are administered by a central federal authority rather than the member states, and in which the previously independent national currencies are merged in a single common currency.[4]

The main disagreement between economists arises not so much from definitions of such stages of integration as from the question whether to integrate at all and if so, how far to go and how to get there. In other words, they are divided on both the ends and the means of integration. For instance, some economists question whether the ends which international integration is supposed to secure (especially income growth and greater economic welfare) might not be better achieved by means other than international integration. They question whether the liberalisation of trade and factor movements will not aggravate capital outflow from lower- to higher-return regions in the integrated area, and thereby accentuate the regional problem within and between nation states. If the reduction of regional disparities within a national economy is a prime aim of government policy, it may be preferable to concentrate policy and resources on the regional integration of the national economy itself. In addition, it can be strongly argued that more effective regional integration and a reduction of regional inequality should be matched by a more conscious effort to equalise income between different social groups and classes (which will tend to be linked to the question of regional income disparities). It is also plausible that such social and regional programmes will be hindered by preoccupation with the trade adjustment problems which may ensue for a national economy committed to international rather than regional and social integration. Even if economists agree that international integration may be desirable on specific political and economic grounds (such as securing a wider freedom of action for the integrated economies in relation to a super-power such as the United States), they may differ on the means of achieving even the first stage of such integration – a free-trade area – and the desirability of proceeding to higher stages of integration at all.

Self-Balance Fiction and Negative Integration

Two main approaches to international economic integration can be distinguished. These have been labelled 'negative' and 'positive' integration, and the distinction is useful as some kind of thread through the maze of the theory.[5] The 'negative' approach basically amounts to the limitation to some countries of the general case for international liberalisation of trade and factor movements, and assumes that liberalisation and policy harmonisation will result in an optimal distribution of resources between labour and capital, between firms and industries; between industry, agriculture and services; between regions within national economies and national economies themselves. This is claimed to occur through the result of several mutually reinforcing effects including (1) the stimulation of competition; (2) greater specialisation in production; (3) increased scale economies in production and distribution; (4) higher productivity and faster growth of output; and (5) strengthened competitiveness in the markets of non-member countries. Stimulation of competition would result from the exposure of previously protected high-cost producers in some economies to lower-cost producers in others, causing them either to reduce their costs and prices or re-allocate resources to other forms of production in which they have a greater comparative advantage. Such specialisation would mean greater scale economies, which would mean higher productivity and faster growth, with labour and capital employed in those activities which earned them their highest feasible rates of return. In general, these factors would increase the competitiveness of the integrated area as a whole in relation to non-member countries.

Superficially, such a self-reinforcing process might well appear a fair description of the dynamics of post-war economic growth in the original six countries of the E.E.C., both during the liberalisation period of the 1950s, and during the decade from 1958 in which they proceeded with the creation of a common market. But a *caveat* is called for of the kind which the E.E.C. Commission, and especially its Competition Directorate, tended to neglect. Basically, such a rationale of the case for integration through liberalisation may fit already well-structured firms in growth industries which have the technical, financial and management capacity to cope with adaptation and change to wider markets and more competitive conditions. But in real-world terms its assumptions do not fit the facts of spatial resource allocation, and it is here that the parallelism with regional economics becomes clearest.

For instance, such a 'negative' model of international integration assumes (1) price competititive micro-economic firms located in national markets, rather than meso-economic and multi-national companies; (2) the availability of scale-economy gains to any firm in the integrated area once it has switched to activities in which it has a comparative advantage; (3) symmetry in factor flows, with labour migrating to high employment demand areas but capital also moving to the higher labour availability areas of emigration; (4) flexible factor returns or the possibility of interregional differentials in wages which unions may not permit for a multi-plant firm; and (5) a self-adjustment in trade and payments between regions (either national or sub-national). In other words, it ignores or assumes away most of the frictions, asymmetries, and imbalances which characterise the modern capitalist economy, and which lie behind the persistence or aggravation of regional problems through the free working of the market mechanism.

The parallelism can be spelled out by considering these main elements of international integration theory in relation to the main features of regional theory. It has already been shown that the main features of meso-economic competition concern not only the degree of brand attachment and market control which puts leading firms in the position of price-makers rather than price-takers, but also the use to which their control of prices can be put as an instrument for prevention of entry to established or new markets, or the elimination of companies which would be economically viable in a competitive world, but which in practice cannot compete with the leading companies' multi-product or multi-national security. It has also been shown that the kind of scale economy available to an owner-managed or single-product company does not compare with the wider scale benefits available to multi-product, meso-economic and multi-national firms, whose resources in terms of R and D, innovation, marketing and growth are incomparable with those of late-starting and more narrowly based micro-economic companies.

The analysis of the structure and size of private-enterprise establishments in the South of Italy shows that the private sector in this major Community region (nearly equal in population size to Belgium and the Netherlands combined) has lost ground to the North of the country in the post-war period. It was characterised by small-scale establishments with a high failure rate, effectively separated from the structure and performance of the rest of the national or Community economy, suggesting both an incapacity to attain to competitive scale advantages through specialisation, as well as difficulties of entry with possible elimination by national and Community leaders in the meso-economic sector.[6]

Both the structure of private enterprise in the South of Italy and the effects of its massive labour emigration also give the lie to the symmetry factor flows assumptions in the 'negative' case for international integration. As already shown, the emigration of nearly two million Italians from the South up to the late 1960s was both to the North and abroad. Abroad, the main labour-inflow area was West Germany, particularly the Oberbayern, Cologne and Darmstadt growth areas.[7] The emigration from the South of Italy constituted virtually the sole source of intra-Community international migration during the 1960s, as opposed to intra-national interregional migration. It was massive by any historical standards, amounting to nearly double the peak South Italian emigration rate of 1911–21,[8] and in this respect certainly corroborates the claim that international liberalisation of factor movements will encourage labour migration *per se*. Moreover, there is sufficient reason to conclude that both the regional economies of the North-west of Italy and the West German growth areas benefited from a raising of their indigenous full-employment ceilings through tapping South Italy's labour-reserve pool, with the previously analysed benefits for these labour-inflow regions of sustained warranted and increased natural rates of growth. But while such growth rates certainly permitted the maintenance of increases in scale, specialisation and productivity gains of the negative integration case, there was no evidence of the counterflow of private North Italian or West German direct investment to the South of Italy which is crucial to the balanced spatial distribution of benefits in an integrated area assumed by the equilibrium models of negative integration theory.

Moreover, while the outflow of so considerable an absolute number of workers from the South of Italy should in principle have altered factor proportions in the region, raising the available capital per worker, the region in fact covered its costs of capital investment through state rather than private expenditure, substantially because its initial backwardness in industrial structure meant that it lacked private companies of sufficient competitiveness to retain or attract savings within the region. In addition, the outflow from the South of Italy of its younger, fitter and more adaptable labour meant a gain for the North-west of the country and for the inflow regions in West Germany, but a senilisation and pauperisation of the remaining labour force, while the West German and other immigration regions abroad secured young men when needed to fill regional employment needs without the capital cost of raising and educating them to the level at which they could learn industrial and other skills after short training periods. Besides which, as already shown, the net outflow of labour from the South of Italy over the period was offset by the natural population increase in the region, so that its absolute population at the end of the 1960s was as high as in 1950.

There are various reasons why firms established in already developed centres should not locate new plant in peripheral regions rather than nearer home. These include inertia, language, common institutions, small marginal savings from nearer rather than more distant locations in the event of both entailing the same labour costs because of nationally agreed union wage levels, and so on. In principle, international integration policies of the E.E.C. kind, which aim at a greater harmonisation of institutions, could in due course eliminate some of the obstacles to the location of subsidiary plant by Community meso-economic leaders in peripheral areas. Moreover, the establishment of a single-currency area in the Community would overcome the exchange risk factor which introduces uncertainty into company planning for small- and medium-sized national firms.

But the very process of harmonisation of policies in an integrated area, which is the essential policy premise of integration of the negative type, simultaneously undermines some of the main gains which multi-national companies can secure through the location of direct investment in member countries of the integrated area, rather than economies outside it. These include the gains from transfer pricing (declaring profits in low-tax rather than high-tax areas), and the bargaining of one national government against another to secure location grants and assistance from the highest bidder (or maintain that one intends to locate elsewhere in order to up national government assistance whether or not the company has decided on the location in the first place). This is in addition to the fact that monetary integration will reduce the main obstacles to international capital migration which obtain in an independent-currency world. And granted the fact that replacement investment on the same site accounts for as much as two-thirds to four-fifths of total net investment in leading industrial economies, plus the inertia and central-area location propensity of firms already in high-income and growth areas, this increased ease of capital movements will tend to increase savings flows from peripheral to central regions in an integrated single currency area.[9]

Besides, to the extent that national trades unions in the integrated area succeed in raising their countervailing power relative to those multi-national companies which are capable of organising the location of plant in peripheral areas, they will tend to insist on the payment of comparable wages for comparable jobs through the area, which in the absence of any other location policy brought to bear on the multi-nationals will reduce the probability of meso-economic location in peripheral regions rather than in other lower wage cost economies outside the integrated area. (This process will tend to occur even when micro-economic local firms can secure lower effective wage agreements from unions, or avoid nationally negotiated minimum-wage legislation, granted the understandable determination of national unions not to allow leading national or multi-national companies to take advantage of a dualistic labour market.)

The negative or equilibrium case for international integration assumes that the specialisation of companies in those activities in which they have a comparative advantage, plus a two-way self-balancing movement in capital flows (savings to high-growth companies and high-growth company direct investment in labour-abundant areas), will ensure that interregional and international payments in the integrated area are automatically balanced. But this breaks down for the same variety of reasons which have been elaborated in previous chapters, including (1) the tendency for a one-way flow of private savings to high-growth companies which stay in high-growth areas rather than locating plant in the labour-abundant emigration areas; (2) the anti-inflationary effects of a raising of the full-employment ceiling in the labour-inflow areas; (3) the possibility of securing lower-cost sites for expansion in areas nearer the centre than the peripheral areas when the original expansion sites become congested to the point at which companies may begin to feel the feedback effect of congestion costs; (4) the very process of scale gains in production and distribution in high-growth areas, which is posited as one of the main cases for international integration, means increasing returns for those areas which already have higher returns than the average, and decreasing relative returns for the originally lower-productivity areas; and (5) the higher rate of productivity gains from the technical progress available to leading companies in more-developed regions.

Labour-abundant regions do have a potential comparative advantage in an integrated area *if* meso-economic companies in more-developed regions find themselves short of labour and consequently locate new plant where labour is abundant. But the focus of national unions on precisely such meso-economic leaders tends to mean that, unless constrained by government policy instruments, the companies will tend not to locate in the labour abundant area, where they would have to pay the same, or closely comparable, wages with those they would cede in a more-developed area. So long as labour migration makes it possible for them to secure the same labour at the same cost at home, they will tend to stay at home, or on the low-cost site nearest the home location. Consequently, structurally disadvantaged micro-economic companies located in problem regions have to compete with the meso-economic leaders in the integrated area and do so on an absolute rather than comparative cost basis. So long as the national government has not agreed to proceed to the stage of monetary union it might try to avoid such absolute disadvantage either for its problem-region companies or its national economy by devaluing the national currency and establishing export prices which are more competitive than in the pre-devaluation period. But in the first place the effect of devaluation is now considerably eroded in the meso-economic and multi-national sector, where firms frequently choose not to reflect the depreciation of one currency in price competition with their own products in other countries. Secondly, in competitive international trade, and some transfer pricing by multi-nationals, devaluation has cumulative disadvantages in terms of raising import prices and worsening national inflation. Thirdly, to the extent that it makes imports less price competitive at home, it thereby partly cushions national micro-economic companies in a manner which, in the absence of successful government restructuring, will only postpone the competitiveness problem. If the government has agreed to proceed to a stage of economic union which involves the harmonisation of policies for restructuring regional development, it will tend to find itself handicapped in fulfilling such policies successfully through restriction of its freedom of action by common policies which apply to all member governments of the union. If it has also agreed to monetary integration, it will have no independent currency to devalue so as to provide a breathing space for such restructuring in the first place. Consequently, over the longer term, it will be likely to find itself subject to an import-led deflation of the von Neumann Whitman kind, in which its export losses reduce its import capacity, as well as defensive investment patterns of the Lamfalussy type.[10]

This catalogue of woe may not occur in precisely the manner described. For one thing, the economies concerned are not simple components in an integration model, operating under *ceteris paribus* conditions, and it cannot be assumed that there will be no government policy responses. The dynamics of growth may be sufficient to assure high absolute income increases even for regions which fall back relatively to the leading growth areas. Otherwise, for historical, social and even psychological reasons, the governments of the fast-growth member states may decide to restrain growth through deflationary policies, even when these have not been made necessary because of an international payments deficit. For instance, this was the case in West Germany in the early 1960s, when the blockade on labour immigration from East Germany with the building of the Berlin Wall showed policy-makers that they were likely to run into tighter labour markets and that their full-employment ceiling would flatten out even though still continuing to rise. Since the experience of hyperinflation following two World Wars had made the Germans far more inflation-conscious than the other members of the Community, this resulted in a series of deflationary measures which considerably reduced the national growth rate, while other member countries such as France, Italy and Belgium maintained higher percentage G.N.P. rates. But the record of cumulative West German revaluations and successive French devaluations since the war is itself an indication of productivity divergences which, within a single-currency area, could only have been offset by a massive and improbable increase in the competitiveness of the French economy.

However, while there are major difficulties in demonstrating the dynamic effects resulting from international integration – not least because of the problem of knowing what would have been the case had integration not occurred – it is a fact that the G.N.P. growth rates of all the member countries of the Community except West Germany increased in the 1960s relative to the 1950s, with an increase in productivity from the mid-1960s onwards which suggests a degree of intra-industry specialisation by companies, scale economies in production and distribution, and other stimulus effects of the kind hypothesised by negative integration theory.[11] Moreover, the Belgian economy, which in the 1950s had been so severely gripped in a low-growth syndrome and 'defensive' investment of the Lamfalussy kind, doubled its annual G.N.P. growth rate after the creation of the E.E.C., and appears to have secured classic 'enterprise' or 'offensive' investment of the kind which it previously had lacked. Besides, the G.N.P. growth rates for these E.E.C. member countries (Belgium, the Netherlands, France and Italy) were very high by any previous or other European capitalist economy standards, between some 4·5 and 5·5 per cent a year. Any national government might well have held that the benefit to any region which could keep up with the national percentage increase, whatever its absolute disparity relative to leading regions, was securing a growth rate which could not have been achieved through an intensification of regional policy instruments and incentives under low national growth rates. Besides, it certainly is true to maintain that one of the principal regional development instruments which has been recommended as a result of the analysis of the previous chapters – locational controls – has little effect in a low-growth economy which is suffering from piecemeal small-scale investment of the Lamfalussy 'defensive' investment type. Negative controls on the expansion of plant in M.D.R.s need sufficient growth to secure a volume of entirely new and potentially footloose plant in the first place.

But, while these allowances are made, there are strong reasons to claim that the process of integration of the negative type aggravates regional problems within nation states, and that the problems will become more acute the higher the stage of integration concerned. A breakdown of the regional growth record and the interregional disparities within the E.E.C. follows in the next chapter, but it is worth mentioning the E.E.C. Commission's own admission that 'an immediate consequence of opening frontiers is an accentuation of tendencies towards geographical concentration'.[12] This can result partly from the resistance exercised by leading national companies to govern- ments which attempt to persuade them to decentralise and locate in peripheral areas during the early stages of in- ternational integration. In the case of Italy leading private- enterprise companies replied that they either could make a success of E.E.C. entry, and cope with the abolition of external tariffs towards other member countries, or organise major new initiatives in the South, but not both. In the French case, the introduction of penalties on expansion in the Paris area has been ignored virtually with impunity not only because the penalties themselves are low, but also because the government has made the national balance of payments its main priority, and has hesitated to squeeze the recalcitrant companies too hard. And these factors are independent of cumulative concentration effects which are likely to become more marked the higher the stage of integration achieved, unless offset by government intervention.

Imbalance Theory and Positive Integration

The 'positive' integration case is based principally on the assumption that the free working of the market through liberalisation may aggravate structural and regional disequilibria, and that government intervention is necessary in order to ensure that international integration avoids net losses rather than gains. Just as the negative integration case shares much in common with the equilibrium theory of spatial location and regional growth, so the positive case shares much with the inverse cumulative disequilibrium and polarisation heritage. While the negative integration case amounts to a limitation to some economies of the case for international liberalisation, or a down-scaling of an international *laissez-faire* model, the positive integration case amounts to an up-grading of the model of the interventionist nation state. The economists who endorse it generally accept that the market mechanism offers efficiency advantages over command or centrally planned economies but stress the social diseconomies which can arise from such a process of decentralised decision-making. In particular, they emphasise the possibility of a divergence in international integration between the private interests of firms and the public interests of major regions and nations in the integrated area. Whereas the negative or liberalisation approach to integration maintains that liberalisation will automatically result in a harmonious adjustment of sectoral and regional structures, the interventionist or positive approach maintains that the public authority, whether national or supra-national, must intervene to ensure such an adjustment. Its analysis of the case for intervention therefore reflects some of the criticism of negative integration which has already been expressed.[13]

In interpreting the role of the E.E.C. or U.S. federal authorities later it is important to bear in mind that the two main approaches to integration do not differ in the sense that the negative case implies an absence of government intervention while the positive case is based on government intervention. The negative or liberalisation approach *does* imply a role for intervention, but this is smaller in scale and different in kind from that which underlies the positive integration case. Basically, negative integration allows that imperfections in the working of the market mechanism can arise from collusive or oligopolistic practices by companies, and therefore claims that strong anti-monopoly or competition policies should be pursued by the authorities responsible for integration. It also maintains that the differentiation of policies between member states in an integrated area can act as an obstacle to the realisation of the gains from liberalisation of trade and factor movements, and as a result recommends the harmonisation of national trade policies as well as internal tariff abolition; the adoption of commonly pursued policies for the reduction of non-tariff barriers to trade; the alignment of taxes on traded goods and services; the harmonisation of capital taxation and the conditions of capital transactions in financial institutions; the harmonisation of state aids to agriculture, industry and services, and the conditions of state intervention in the structure of production; the alignment of exchange rates in the pre-monetary integration stages, and the pursuit of common or non-conflicting monetary policies; an alignment of indirect wages, subsidies or social-security benefits of the kind which can affect cost structures between firms in different economies; and, most importantly in this context, the harmonisation of regional policies and an alignment of state aid for regional development.

In principle, whereas the advocates of negative integration tend to maintain that more integration is better than less, the advocates of positive integration should hold the reverse. In other words, while the negative integration case is based on the assumption that the free working of the market mechanism will, in the long run, eliminate disparities between countries and regions, the positive integration case maintains that the longer the run the greater the problems for countries and regions may become, with cumulative divergences in productivity, income and employment. The negative integration case maintains that there will be gains from successively higher stages of integration. Thus a customs union is held to be an improvement on a free-trade area because it will avoid distortions of competition which can arise from some countries having lower or higher tariffs towards third countries than others. Similarly, it maintains that the liberalisation of factor movements is essential to avoid distortions in the allocation of labour and capital in different countries and regions, thereby preferring a common market to a customs union. But inasmuch as it claims that it will be necessary to harmonise those government policies which affect trade and factor movements between countries, it recommends progress to the higher stage of economic union, with the harmonisation of policies between member states. Ultimately, and as a logical outcome of the premises on which the case is based, it maintains that monetary integration will be necessary to secure an optimal spatial distribution of trade and factors of production through the integrated area.

The reverse positive integration case is based on different assumptions concerning the free working of the market and its 'policing' by either member governments or a supra-national authority. Basically, the advocates of the positive integration case maintain that even liberalisation of trade within a free-trade area may aggravate rather than reduce balance-of-payments and growth problems between member countries, and that it may be important for a member state of a free-trade area to resist the abandonment of the use of external tariffs as a trade adjustment instrument, which would be necessary in progressing to the second stage of a common external tariff for the integrated area. Basing their case on observed asymmetries in labour and capital flows, plus the cumulative divergences which arise from reinforced scale benefits to already leading firms in developed areas, they may also resist progress to the third stage of a common market, maintaining that an initially disadvantaged country within the area may need to maintain controls on capital exports in order to improve its domestic competitiveness towards the other countries in the integrated area. If they accept that there is a case for the first three stages of integration (free-trade area, customs union and common market), they may only do so by insisting that any degree of economic union (stage four) should permit a high degree of differentiation in the policy instruments employed by member states to ensure the successful adaptation of their problem industries and regions to the higher growth opportunities possible through a larger market. Inasmuch as the advocates of the positive integration case tend to become more reluctant the higher the stage of integration proposed, the main difference between them and the advocates of negative integration concerns the final stage of monetary integration, where they maintain that it is crucial that member states should retain the capacity to alter exchange rates to maintain the price competitiveness of exports in the area, which is impossible with a single currency. (This issue may become less relevant as awareness increases that the meso-economic and multi-national firms which now dominate the top half of European industry increasingly discount exchange-rate changes in their planning of location and production in Europe.) Devaluation becomes less significant the greater the continuing trend to multi-national rather than international trade.

The awareness of the stubbornness of regional problems within nation states, and the difficulty of reducing regional disparities even with complete freedom of domestic policy instruments, has played a crucial part in the resistance of several advocates of positive integration to monetary integration. They are aware that devaluation has its handicaps in improving the competitiveness of a national economy's exports, but also are aware of the 'breathing space' which it can permit, and of the extent to which it can at least be employed with other policies as a means of preventing an increase in national and regional unemployment of the kind which could emerge in an 'import-led' decline of the von Neumann Whitman kind. They also take account of the very considerable complexity in the task of improving productivity through restructuring policies, and the substantial period of time which may be necessary to make progress with such policies. They lay emphasis on the fact that regional problems may differ significantly between different areas in an internationally integrated community, and that effective regional policies may demand flexible and different instruments for different areas (such as a declining coal field in an otherwise relatively prosperous region; pockets of seasonal unemployment in tourist resorts; an isolated shipyard in an area too far from main employment centres to allow workers to commute to new jobs rather than being forced to emigrate; the unemployment of inner core areas in what otherwise constitute the highest employment and average *per capita* income centres in the economy, and so on).

Politics, Regions and Integration

The differences between the negative and positive interpreta-
tions of international integration do not imply a mutual
acceptance of the case for integration as such. As can be seen
from the previous analysis, the greater the scepticism of the
benefits claimed from the negative liberalisation case, the
greater the resistance not only to higher stages of integration,
but also possibly to any integration at all, including the first stage
of a free-trade area. In general, the two types of analysis also
entail different political assumptions about the way in which
both the economy and society should be organised. The negative
case is economistic in the sense that it assumes that the means of
economic liberalisation will automatically secure optimal welfare
ends provided that the market is sufficiently well policed by the
responsible authorities. The interventionist positive integration
analysis may accept liberalisation as a means to certain specific
economic ends, but in general will entail a much wider role for
the directly elected political authority and its responsibility to
particular social and economic groups in the national economy,
as well as to particular sub-national regional authorities where
these already exist.

The negative and positive integration cases cannot be
distinguished simply on Right–Left political grounds. Historically, the negative case can trace its antecedents through general
free trade and liberalisation theory stemming from Adam
Smith, and finding its more recent reincarnation in the social
market philosophy of Eucken and Böhm in West Germany.[14] To
this extent it could well be described as the integration
philosophy of liberal capitalism. But the positive integration case
is not exclusively a property of anti-capitalists or socialists. Its
main practical advocacy in the E.E.C. case to date has been by
successive Gaullist and neo-Gaullist governments, which are
quite explicitly capitalist even if their capitalism is interventionist
in kind rather than neo-liberal in the German fashion. It is the
French within the Commission which have pushed most strongly
for the establishment of a Community planning framework and
Commission endorsement of the case for greater intervention to
cope with structural and regional problems, co-ordinated on an
internationalist basis through mutual agreement by Community

governments. In Britain many socialists and many members of the Labour Party have condemned E.E.C. integration on theoretical, practical and political grounds. But others have argued that there are substantial net benefits to be secured through some kind of closer integration between the British and E.E.C. economies, provided adequate safeguards are maintained for avoidance of net losses in major areas for which national governments at present remain responsible, such as regional policy. Their qualified support for some degree of international integration also tends to be based in part on political–economic factors such as the difficulty of securing genuine economic sovereignty in a national economy which is subject to 'play off' by multi-national companies and the increasingly one-sided nature of the so-called 'special relationship' with the United States. It also tends to be based on the assumption that the Rome Treaty provisions do not themselves concern the nature of private or public ownership of the means of production, or the use of new public enterprise as the spearhead of future regional development in member states of the Community – which is legitimate granted the expanded use to which State companies have been put in regional development in Italy since the Community began.

Economic and Monetary Union

The regional implications of monetary union can be illustrated by considering the case for a national sub-region turning back the clock and making a unilateral declaration of monetary independence, thus establishing its own currency. The Mundell 'optimum currency' area is such a region, defined as an area in which there is effective factor mobility. But granted the spatial inelasticity of labour migration, Mundell admitted that this could result in a region being defined so narrowly as to include every minor pocket of unemployment, which should apparently have its own independent currency. As he commented, rejecting the theoretical argument he had developed, this 'hardly appeals to common sense'.[15] But the larger the problem region concerned, the stronger the case for an independent currency becomes on both Mundell's grounds and those which have been argued earlier in this chapter. McKinnon has argued that there is a strong case for giving the Appalachian states in the United States an independent currency, and there could certainly be claimed to be a similar case for giving an independent currency to the major problem region in the E.E.C. – the South of Italy.[16] But as already pointed out, such a case depends substantially on the region concerned already having a sufficiently modern economic structure to be able to take advantage of the gains in export-price competitiveness which the possibility of devaluing an independent currency would permit. Price competitiveness alone is no great help if the quality of exportable products or services is so poor that they cannot compete even at lower unit prices with other exports or domestic import substitutes in the integrated area. It certainly does not help if the regional economy lacks the productive capacity to substitute for the higher-cost imports following devaluation.

It is here again that political factors are important, and influence the case either for putting the clock back and establishing an independent currency, or putting it forward and merging previously independent currencies in a single mone-tary unit. One of the main losses likely from the introduction of an independent currency in a region which already cannot cover the bulk of its capital accumulation from domestic resources is the ending of regional aid from other regions in the national economy if it decides to risk the consequences, setting up its own currency and becoming effectively a new nation state. This is no longer a purely theoretical question granted the nationalist pressures for an independent Scotland breaking away from the rest of the United Kingdom. It may be more theoretical in re-verse, in the example of the E.E.C. and the acceptance by its governments of a programme for monetary union, however long term. One of the main reasons for a national government to hesi-tate before taking the leap into a single-currency area is the darkness clouding the nature of the assistance which it might be able to secure from other member states in the event of not being able to cover its import needs by exports, and starting the downward path of import-led decline. And this is one of the least clear issues in the current E.E.C. programme. The advocates of E.E.C. monetary integration maintain that a federal Community authority, with its own budget, would be able to fulfil such transfers, checked and supervised by a directly elected

European federal parliament. But one of the main problems in regional development is not so much the availability of funds for development, but ensuring both that they are employed productively and in such a way as to ensure the recovery of a balanced regional trade and growth. And this entails not only structural and institutional questions, but also the question of the role of meso-economic multi-national capital in the integrated area.

If such leading companies are completely free in their location choice, serious problems are raised in terms of promoting the growth of problem regions. Yet the powers necessary for a federal authority to be able to impose locational controls on such companies would have to be more extensive than those at present employed in an integrated economy such as the United States, which can call on the experience of 200 years of federal authority. It could mean refusing expansion permission not only to British firms in the Midlands and South-east, but also to certain Dutch and West German firms anywhere in their national territories. Such powers are unlikely in the foreseeable future and, in any case, are not clearly justifiable relative to alternative national policies for coping with the 'regional problem', possibly supplemented at the international level.

Resource transfer of an indirect kind through government incentives to regional development, and direct expenditure in problem regions through State companies or on infrastructural projects, can do a substantial amount to prevent a deterioration in the regional disparities in a national economy or an economy in the pre-federal stages of integration, as the following analysis of the pattern of regional distribution in the E.E.C. to date indicates. But more must be done to ensure a marked reduction in the relative disparities between E.E.C. regions through the 1970s, particularly if the end of the decade or the beginning of the 1980s is to be marked by the introduction of a single Community currency.

CHAPTER 5

REGIONS VERSUS EUROPE[1]

It has been argued that the free working of the market mechanism will tend to aggravate rather than reduce regional disparities unless state intervention can countervail the inherent imbalance of market forces. This allows for the exception of special comparative advantage in agriculture, forestry, raw materials or what might be called 'economic geography'.

A critical premise for the effectiveness of conventional development policy is a higher over-all macro-economic rate of growth. (In meso-economic regional planning, forward investment through leading firms, modernising capacity through location in problem regions and areas, can qualify the high macro growth condition at least in the medium term, depending on the real effectiveness of meso–macro linkage in investment planning at the national level.)

It should be clear that a high macro-economic growth rate is not a sufficient condition for regional development under conditions of unequal competition and cumulative imbalance characteristic of capitalist market economies (that is unequal development both within industries and between regions). Similarly, for the reasons just given, it need not be a necessary condition for effective meso-economic planning if governments have the power to harness the forward planning of regionally mobile public enterprise in development projects which are long term in character and act as a counter to the private trade cycle.

Regional Imbalance in the Community

None the less, under conventional development policies, high macro-economic growth is a necessary condition for the generation of a volume of entirely new plant which can be located in problem regions and areas. In the 'long boom' of the twenty years from 1950 in most of the original six member countries of the E.E.C., such a sustained macro-economic expansion made it possible for conventional micro-economic policies to exert some influence on regional location. In aggregate terms the performance was not that remarkable. Leading regions gained relative to lagging regions in the Six. However, some of the least-developed regions gained in terms of income per head, not least through the convenient pheno-menon (for the statisticians) that the resident population was reduced through relative emigration.

For instance, income per head in the South of Italy grew by 5 per cent a year from 1960 to 1969, against only 4 per cent a year in the North. Before the establishment of the Community in 1958, income per head in the South had grown by less than in the more-developed North.

In Germany the previously most backward regions (the Centre–South and the Eastern Order) reduced their gap in output per head compared with the more developed West and North, consistently catching up over the period from 1958 to 1968.

Over the same period the previously most backward regions in the Netherlands (the North and the South) also reduced their gap in income per head with the more developed East and West regions, with the East of the country falling back from second to third place.

In Belgium the country's three regions grew at a high and almost equal annual G.D.P. – 8·7 per cent for the Brussels and Flanders regions, and 7·1 per cent for the Walloon region, which fell from second to third place.

In France only one region which began the post-E.E.C. period with a proportion of G.D.P. *per capita* lower than the national average grew more slowly than the national average G.D.P. growth rate from 1962 to 1967 and even this region, the South-West, grew by 7·9 per cent a year.[2]

What emerges from these figures is a convergence effect, even if very slight. Also, the absolute growth rates of the more backward regions have been impressive. On the other hand, this does not mean either that Community policy has been respons-ible for the improvement of backward regions, or that harmon-isation of national policies will help avoid an increasing divergence in the future. In practice, the slight improvement of the position of the most backward regions has been the result of (1) intensified national policy based on state enterprise in the case of Italy, dating from 1957, and (2) massive depopulation of some rural areas, especially in France, which helps improve the *per capita* income or product figures in those cases where government policy has had any effect in offsetting a syphoning of capital or enterprise back to the metropolitan centres.

The disparities between main regions in the Community are still very substantial. All Italian regions have income *per capita* levels below the Community average, with Piedmont, Val d'Aosta and Liguria registering an average level only one-half that of the Paris region (the highest level in the Six). Campania, Molise, Sicily, Sardinia, Apulia, Basilicata and Calabria have incomes *per capita* of less than one-quarter the Paris level. All the Belgian and West German regions have income *per capita* higher than the Community average, and the Netherlands East region is the only one below it. Again, all French regions except Paris are below the Community average, with less than one-half the income *per capita* level of the Paris region. In other words, there are still major income disparities not only within member countries but also between them as a whole.[3] Of course, the income or product indices are not the only indications of major regional backwardness. The other main indices include the proportion of economically active population (activity rate), unemployment, the distribution of working population, the distribution of jobs for matching skills, and high rates of net emigration. As would be expected, within the E.E.C., leading regions in terms of income-product *per capita* show the highest activity rates in 1969 and the lagging regions the lowest; the disparity ranged from nearly 50 per cent for the Paris region to just over 30 per cent for the South of Italy as a whole, and only just more than 25 per cent for Sicily and Sardinia. This is despite the fact that agricultural under-employment swells the activity rates for the main agricultural regions; this helps to bring West and South France higher up the scale.[4]

Italy included the highest unemployment regions in the Community in 1969, with all regions in the South showing registered unemployment levels of about 3 per cent. Both these levels and those of the next highest unemployment regions in

the Community in the same year (Mediterranean France and
Liege at 1·7 and 1·6 per cent respectively) are low in
comparison with the July 1972 figures for regional unemployment in the United Kingdom, which showed 8·4 per cent (male)
and 3·5 per cent (female) in Scotland; 6·7 per cent (male) and
2·7 per cent (female) in Wales; 7·8 per cent (male) and 2·2 per
cent (female) in North England, and 10·2 per cent (male) and
0·0 per cent (female) in Northern Ireland. However, some
doubt should be placed on the comparability of these figures
granted the different bases of calculation, and the extent of
disguised unemployment in agriculture in the South of Italy and
the South of France.[5]

The distribution of agricultural employment by main country
and region in the original Six members of the Community shows
marked disparities between Belgium, the Netherlands and
Germany on the one hand, and Italy and France on the other. In
Germany the national share of population in agriculture was 3·6
per cent in 1969, and the share for the two most agricultural
regions (Niedersachsen and Rheinland-Pfalz) was 5·2 per cent.
In the Netherlands the North region had just more than twice
the national average population in agriculture (but this was only
5·7 per cent against the national 2·8 per cent). Belgium had no
region with more than 3·7 per cent of population in agriculture,
against a national average of only 2·2 per cent. South Italy and
South and West France showed the highest proportions of
population in agriculture, all over 10 per cent of total regional
population, with an average of 13·6 per cent for the South of
Italy, against only just more than 8 per cent of regional
population employed in industry.[6]

The employment problems of the South of Italy are massive
enough even if no allowance is made for (1) the effects of
workers migrating to the North and other countries; (2) the
quality, type and distribution of industrial employment in the
region; and (3) the industrial investment which has resulted
from Italian government policy measures. Migrants from the
region between 1950 to 1967 totalled about 1,700,000 persons,
yet this outflow to the North of the country and abroad was
equalled by the natural population increase; the total regional
population increased to over 20 million (nearly equal to that of
two member states of the Community combined – Belgium and

the Netherlands). Emigration of the younger, more skilled and better adaptable labour to other national and Community regions has handicapped economic development in some areas in the region. Despite such high total emigration figures, the relative unresponsiveness of southern Italian labour to interregional and international income differences has been the highest in the Community and resulted in the persistence of not only interregional dualism between North and South Italy but also intra-regional dualism within the South where isolated areas of development exist with little 'pull effect' on the rest.

The fact that there is now evidence of a slight interregional convergence between Italy and the rest of the Community might suggest that the worst is past and that this will be the future pattern for old and new members of the Community. But, as a background to evaluating what kind of future policy instruments both Britain and the Community as a whole may need in the future, it is worth considering the Community's own estimates of the kind of regional growth rate necessary if any significant impact is to be made on regional income differences over given time-periods. Taking a fifteen-year period and a Community growth rate of 4 per cent a year it would be necessary for a region with one-half the highest Community income level to grow by 9 per cent a year to catch up, and a region with one-third the highest Community level 12 per cent a year. It clearly may not be considered politically or economically necessary to secure absolute interregional equality rather than a reduced disparity, but the kind of growth necessary to do so shows that there is very little cause for congratulation. This is particularly the case since the rates necessary for the backward regions to catch up over the same time period rise to 11 per cent and over 14 per cent if the Community average growth is taken as 6 rather than 4 per cent a year. At present, Community regions with less than one-half the income *per capita* level of the leading regions include Piedmont and Liguria in the North of Italy, and all the French regions except Paris, while most of the regions in the South of Italy have income *per capita* levels less than one-quarter those in the most-developed region in the Community.

Common Policies versus State Power

Until the Paris summit meeting of December 1974 there was virtually no Community regional policy of the 'positive' integration type, that is a common policy jointly agreed by member governments and to be administered on their behalf, with common funds, by the Commission. This is not to say that the Community did not previously have common policies with a major regional impact; in the case of the Common Agricultural Policy it clearly did. Besides which, the formal power of the Commission to vet and forbid certain categories of aid to industry had considerable regional implications in principle, if not much in practice. But for a variety of reasons the admission of the need for a positive regional policy as such has taken time to develop, and member governments are still in disagreement over more than very general principles for such a policy.

The Rome Treaty's emphasis on public expenditure for regional development was negative rather than positive. Its main rules on competition stipulated that

> any aid granted by a member state or by means of state resources in any form whatsoever which threatens to distort competition by favouring certain undertakings or the production of certain goods shall, in so far as it affects trade between member states, be deemed incompatible with the Common Market.

State aids of 'a social character' or to make good damage from natural disasters 'or other extraordinary events' were to be allowed, as were 'aids to promote the economic development of regions where the standard of living is abnormally low or where there is serious unemployment'. And, as with the Paris Treaty of the Coal and Steel Community, a Social Fund was established to assist in the retraining of workers who had lost their jobs as the result of the impact of integration. This was the case, for example, with old industries running down and new ones opening up. The European Investment Bank was also set up to facilitate both the financing of projects in less-developed regions and projects of common interest to member states which by their size or nature could not be entirely financed by the various means available to individual member states.[7] None the less, the European Investment Bank is a bank proper rather than a regional aid agency. In other words, in contrast with the substantial development grants on investment given by the British government, it offers only interest-rate concessions on loans which have to be repaid. Also, according to the Rome Treaty, the authority to decide whether to grant state aids for regional development was to lie with the Commission rather than with member governments or their officials. And the apprehension at the Commission's possible use of its powers was shown by Italy's insistence that it be allowed a special protocol exception to the Treaty to permit it to implement the relatively low scale and anyway indirect development policies for the Mezzogiorno envisaged in the Vanoni Programme of 1955.[8]

Community officials, some government ministers of member countries and other participants in the drafting of the Treaty itself explain this in a variety of ways. They draw attention to the fact that the member governments had never before been bound by minor articles of international agreements when this did not suit them, and that no one expected the Rome Treaty to be implemented clause by clause in any particularly different way. Most of the provisions of the Paris Treaty had been broken or neglected in practice by the time the Rome Treaty was signed. Moreover, the Treaty itself was concerned with the establishment of a customs union in the first instance, and the competition rules had a trade emphasis, as made plain by the fact that aids would only be deemed incompatible where they affected trade between member states. This was a provision difficult to establish in the first place, quite apart from enforcing it on member governments who remained the primary sovereign powers in the Community, and on whose authority the Commission itself ultimately depended. This is illustrated by the fact that the Commission 'required' the Italian government in 1959 to reveal the subsidy element in the I.R.I. State Holding Company's Taranto steel plant – in the instep of the Italian peninsula. Yet despite much huffing by the Competition Commissioner concerned, with frequent reference to his 'powers' under the Rome Treaty, the Italian government simply sat on the request. The figures were only revealed *thirteen* years later, on I.R.I.'s choice, in an independent academic study.[9]

It is important to grasp that the implemention of any Commission decision depends on the readiness of the member states to accept it. This power might have been challenged by the progressive adoption of majority voting in the Council of Ministers from 1966 as envisaged in the Treaty, but the French blocked that by their walk-out from the Council in June 1965, and their agreement to proceed with Community business in January 1966 only after the other member countries accepted that majority voting in the Council would not be employed in cases of 'important national interest' (the Luxembourg Declaration).

In practice, virtually nothing has been decided by majority vote since that date in the Council other than minor Commission appointments. The Heath–Pompidou first summit also affirmed the determination to maintain the unanimity principle in the Council. Moreover, the growing role of the Committee of Permanent Representatives (Ambassadors to the Community) has meant that national officials have increasingly brought influence to bear on the Commission before Commission proposals went to the Council. This has indicated in advance what a major or minor state would consider 'of important national interest'.

Implications for British Regional Policy

The results of this compromise in the nature of Community decision-making are important for British regional policy in the Community. They show that Britain need not accept aspects of Community policy which it decides will be a disadvantage to its regional policy measures, *provided* its government and officials show sufficient determination. In practice, the blocking unanimity vote in the Council of Ministers on general issues of policy can be exercised to reinforce or override new Commission proposals which were considered against the regional interest of a member state. Of course, this is not as adequate a safeguard for national regional policy as a revision of the Rome Treaty. It also demands a degree of determined Gaullism of a kind which some British Cabinets may show, while others may not. It certainly is not enough to argue simply from precedent, despite the fact that the precedents are massive, and reflect the real need of national governments to protect regional interests against free-market metaphysicians in some directorates of the Commission. Community regional policy has been substantially stalemated since early 1966, by the French refusal that year to agree to 'co-ordination' of regional policies rather than 'comparison',[10] and hardly qualified in practice by subsequent more 'European' statements of intent from Chancellor Schmidt or President Giscard d'Estaing. Nor has this position been substantially modified by the agreement to limit investment grants in 'central' areas of the Community to 20 per cent, since this does not prevent other measures than investment grants being employed to bring effective regional aid well over 20 per cent of total costs. Recent Commission proposals for Community regional policy include a projected special regional policy committee, but this French proposal would put that committee 'under the guidance of the Council' – and therefore nation-state power – rather than the Commission.

It is wrong to assume automatically that there is any major incompatibility between British regional policy recently adopted or in force, and those adopted in the Community. In some cases there have been significant differences in the scale of funds permitted by Britain in relation to particular projects. For instance, regional investment grants were raised to 45 per cent by the Labour Government in 1967 – at the same time more than twice the level of nominal grants available in the Six. But in some areas of the South of Italy the combination of investment grants, depreciation allowances, interest-rate concessions and so on has amounted to total aid equivalents which have approached this (two-thirds of the cost of setting up a project in Sardinia, with one-half the costs in Sicily, are met by the government). In general, grants for regional development are lower on the mainland of the South of Italy, and in France the highest grant available is 20 per cent in the 'growth centre' *métropoles d'équilibre*, with only 12 per cent grants available elsewhere throughout the French South and West development areas. Certainly the present British Government's establishment of grant levels of 22 per cent in special development areas, with 20 per cent levels for development areas in general, intermediate areas and 'derelict' areas is in line with current French practice. Also, the special problems of Northern Ireland – the only region in the Community with a violent political dimension to its regional problem other than the Flemish Walloon dispute in Belgium – should justify greater grants in view of the greater scale and intractability of its problems. In general, the Commission is on record as preferring grants, which it considers 'transparent', to depreciation allowances, which are more opaque.[11]

The principle behind the British Regional Employment Premium (development area wage subsidy) has been accepted, or at least tolerated, by the Competition Directorate of the Commission, with the introduction of special assistance measures in the South of Italy in August 1968, whereby industrial firms employing more than 35 people are entitled to a reduction in the considerable social-security obligations which they are nominally obliged to pay for employees, with the state making up the difference.

Such special assistance measures for firms in difficulties were paralleled by the British Labour Government provision in 1975 to pay up to £10 a head of the wage bill of firms in scheduled Development Areas, provided that the firms could demonstrate the prospect of medium-term viability.

In the event of any Community country or the Commission maintaining that British Industrial Development Certificates (I.D.C.s) are incompatible – as location controls – with the 'capital liberalisation' and 'freedom of establishment' provisions of the Treaty, the British government could possibly secure the support of the French government, which operates a system of financial penalties on expansion in the Paris area (even if they are too low to bite with rigour) and also of the Italian government which has used various controls over the location of state enterprise in the South since July 1957 – three months after the signature of the Rome Treaty.

As for the National Enterprise Board and the Planning Agreements System, evidence (see pp.91–2) shows that both have been accepted in principle by the current Commissioner for Regional Policy – George Thomson – even if this is not enough to ensure that the Competition Directorate will not regard them as violating the innocence of its already lost world of equal competition, or to ensure that Mr Thomson could carry the whole Commission with him in endorsing the regional implications of the Labour Government's industrial strategy since 1974.

Monetary Integration and Regional Disintegration

In other words, there is no reason for a determined government in the E.E.C. to fear that a sabre-toothed Commission will be able to demolish its national regional policies. On the other hand, the national government must both be determined in the first place, and in a relatively strong over-all bargaining position in the Community if it is to overcome opposition both by the Commission and by other member states. There also is considerable reason to maintain that the effectiveness of national policies for regional development will be undermined the higher the stage of Community integration attempted. And this problem will become more serious if Chancellors and Finance Ministers think they can make instant history by proceeding with monetary integration without economic policies ensuring a capacity to offset the imbalance trends in regional growth and trade. It has been seen that the abolition of independent currencies means abolishing the possibility of devaluation. Competing in such a situation means securing comparable productivity levels throughout the single-currency area simply in order to maintain the previous income and welfare distribution. But in practice it is the developed regions whose industries are best able to adjust to the situation. The impact of monetary union is likely to improve the productivity of already leading regions in relation to the rest.

The evidence of the Community before monetary integration is highly instructive in this respect. The high rates of growth of G.N.P., and the minor convergence effect for the more backward regions, was achieved not only during a period of cheap oil, but also over a period in which the West German authorities successively revalued, the French successively devalued, the Italians introduced a disguised devaluation, and, in the end, some of the major partners floated. The relative positions of France, West Germany and Italy are particularly important, inasmuch as West Germany includes the main 'central' areas of labour inflow to the Community. France benefited on a much smaller scale from labour migration, raising the full-employment ceiling of its own central area, than did either West Germany as a whole or the inflow area of North-West Italy. In general it can be allowed that the abolition of independent currencies might raise productivity where previous fears of exchange-rate changes had acted as obstacles to investment and trade. Also its relative irreversibility in relation to other policy instruments might promote long-term investment which otherwise would not take place. But there is no guarantee that this newly promoted investment will be located in problem regions rather than central areas, and to the extent that monetary integration is a stimulus to a national economy it is likely to increase rather than decrease regional disparities for the reasons outlined in previous chapters

As already indicated, regional structure is crucial in two main senses in regional development:

(a) *Intra*-sectoral structure, or the capacity of the regional firm to cope with national and multi-national competition, and
(b) *Inter*-sectoral structure, or the distribution of jobs between high and low productivity and income sectors.

The structural question becomes even more important in the event of countries in an integrated area deciding either to move to monetary union, or introduce independent regional currencies. If a region or nation state lacks the kind of structure capable of favourably reacting to the lowering of export prices which devaluation would permit, and if devaluation would so raise its import prices over a wider range of goods as to offset the export advantage, the case for an independent currency is small. The size of the region itself will influence these factors. But now, and more importantly, they also will be influenced by the hold of multi-national companies on the regional economy, and the extent to which they discount exchange-rate changes in European planning.

Where does this leave us? For one thing it indicates clearly enough that the case for proceeding to monetary union is not at all self-evident. In capital mobility, the multi-national firms which now dominate the most mobile industries in the Community 'integrated' the European market years ago in both direct investment and financial terms through locating subsidi-

aries in different Community countries and through Euromar-
ket borrowing. In labour mobility, it is clear that only Italy is a
significant provider of labour, and that intra-Community
international migration is otherwise insignificant. Moreover,
both are relatively insignificant when compared with the far
higher level of immigration to the Community from non-
member countries, such as Turkey, Greece, Yugoslavia, Spain
and Portugal.

In practice, the question of monetary union cannot be
generalised from a regional viewpoint without reference to
particular criteria. As they emerge from the previous analysis,
they include:

(a) The initial productive structure of the nation states to be
integrated in the single-currency area.

(b) The previous tendency to convergence or divergence in the
proposed single-currency area, and in particular the rate of any
convergence effect.

(c) The relative institutional integration of capital markets in the
area before and after monetary integration.

(d) The relative unemployment and under-employment in
problem regions.

(e) The rate, direction and consequences of international labour
migration before monetary integration.

(f) The possible stimulus effects to investment and productivity
for medium-sized micro-economic firms in particular regions
through monetary integration.

(g) The ratio of micro-economic regional to meso-economic
multi-national firms in the area to be integrated and their
relative locational concentration.

While the lines to be drawn must indeed be relative rather than
absolute, it is not necessary to go to extremes to find something
to make a sensible fit with the facts. Perhaps the following would
fulfil these constraints:

(1) At least the main member states of the old Community
(France, Italy and Germany) plus the United Kingdom, and also
Benelux as a single area, possess a sufficient productive

structure and adaptive capacity to be able to benefit from independent currencies and exchange-rate changes.

(2) The previous convergence trend of the Six and their constituent regions has been clear but not so high or fast as to indicate that the relative speed of labour and capital movements will not be increased with monetary integration, particularly since the change will be sharp in relation to the more gradual evolution of initially 'distance protected' regions in the United States.

(3) The European capital market has been 'integrated' for some time through both multi-national location of subsidiaries and by the Eurodollar and Eurobond markets to which meso-economic firms are the main providers of funds, and from which they are the chief beneficiaries. In other words, for the big-league, meso-economic firms, European monetary integration has already been a fact for some time. The new meso-economic location since the formation of the Community, as indicated by the previously cited figures on foreign multi-nationals, shows a marked concentration in the most-developed areas of the Community. Meanwhile, real interpenetration of financial markets, at the micro-economic or small-league firm level, in Western Europe has yet to begin in terms of mutual listing of members' companies and a balancing of the London banks' activities abroad by the activities of continental banks. In general these factors will be likely to attract hitherto untapped sources of savings away from lower to higher productivity and profit areas.

(4) Regional unemployment in the main peripheral areas of the Community has been reduced since 1950, but the rate of reduction has not accelerated in the 1960s. There are major obstacles to such improvement at present; in key cases such as in the South of Italy the share of employment in manufacturing fell during the period 1950 to 1968, and the fall was significant in modern as well as in traditional manufacturing. After 1968, national growth of employment in manufacturing fell over-all, save for the public-sector State Holdings, which expanded investment against the private-sector trend and located their new plant in the problem region of the South.[12] Unless government or Community policy is able to ensure an increase in the rate of employment in such areas by such means after monetary integration they may well form a persistently under-

developed periphery to the growth taking place in the central
areas, which can expect to benefit from a rate of investment
higher than the rate of indigenous savings through not only
present capital flows but an acceleration of these flows after
monetary integration.

(5) The out-migration of labour from the South of Italy has not
reduced total regional population nor has it increased productivity in agriculture. Indeed it has raised the output potential
of the North-west region of the Italian economy and the central
areas in the rest of the Community. It appears clear from the
fact that the Paris region has increased its lead on the rest of the
French and Community economy that the same effect has
occurred through the transfer of agricultural-rural labour to
industrial and service employment in the metropolis. This
problem could be intensified to the extent that the 1970s and
1980s are likely to show a higher rate of new technologies which
reduce labour requirements.

(6) Depending on the depth and duration of the world recession
following the OPEC oil price increases since 1973, it seems clear
that, without offsetting national and Community policies, it is
likely that any stimulus effect from monetary integration would
reinforce the centripetal capital flows in the Community and
swing the narrow balance from the slight convergence effect in
per capita incomes, evident in the 1960s, to a divergence effect
possibly stronger than that of the 1950s.

(7) Monetary integration would have a considerable effect on
many micro-economic non-multi-national firms in depriving
them of the gain in foreign trade competitiveness made possible
through devaluation. At the same time, it would not much
increase their access to foreign capital, since this is already
available through the Eurodollar and Eurobond markets. The
irony lies in the fact that such small firms in the micro-economic
sector in any case do not contribute much to international trade
relative to their share of total exporting firms, since this trade is
dominated by the multi-nationals in the meso-economic sector.
For instance, in 1973, out of a total of some 10,000 regularly
exporting firms in Britain, 220 companies accounted for
two-thirds of direct exports, 75 firms for one-half of such
exports, and nearly 30 firms for two-fifths.[13] Further, since the
international credit rating of micro-economic firms depends in

large part on bankers' or investors' estimates of their capacity to survive in unequal competition against the meso-economic, multi-national sector, this would not be changed to any considerable extent by monetary integration and they therefore would not benefit much from it. If anything, such a high degree of integration would decrease the protection which they secure in local markets relative to the meso-economic, multi-national league.

False Hopes from a Regional Fund

What of other aspects of Community policy?

The Community has now introduced a Common Regional Fund, supplementing the present aid through the Coal and Steel Community and loans available for problem regions through the European Investment Bank. But such a Fund is more a delusion and snare than an instrument capable of transforming the prospects of Europe's problem regions. As already indicated in Chapter 2, there is considerable evidence that the increasing market power of leading companies permits them profits through multi-national operations which reduce the pull effect of regional aids. Basically, such firms are tending to locate their relatively labour intensive production in such countries as South Korea, Taiwan, the Philippines, Mexico and Brazil, where labour costs can be 5 to 25 per cent of European labour costs. This means that such firms are the most suitable for regional development (relatively labour intensive in a regionally mobile sector), but least susceptible to incentives of a cash kind. (See Chapter 2.)

In fact there is some evidence that the Commission's regional directorate are aware of the potential limitations of the proposed Community Regional Fund, and are seeking means of devising more effective policies. In evidence to the House of Commons Expenditure Committee in February 1973, the Commissioner for Regional Affairs, George Thomson, stated that he was attracted by the possibility of securing more use within the Community of two measures which had already shown their potential in national regional policy.[14] The first of these is the Programme Contracts or Planning Agreements System, which has been operated by the authorities in France,

Italy and Belgium since 1968. This is a procedure by which the government secures advance information from leading companies on a whole range of activities relevant to the outcome of their respective national and regional plans. It includes anticipated price increases, investment and technology promotion, job creation, contribution to national trade, and regional location. It is unlikely that national governments would be willing to relinquish such scrutiny and leverage on leading firms to the Commission, especially for national firms over which they still have a high degree of control. But there is considerable scope for securing closer liaison between the Commission and national authorities in the crucial case of multi-national companies, where national governments already have seen their planning powers eroded by the access open to such companies for the location of plant outside the Community, or in other Community countries.

The other main regional instrument in which George Thomson expressed interest was the use of public enterprise as a direct instrument for regional development, through State Holding Companies. As already indicated, the most notable case in which such public enterprise has already achieved considerable success is the problem region of the South of Italy. From 1957 to 1968 State Holding Companies were in principle obliged to locate at least 60 per cent of their total investment in new plant in the South. This in spite of a less than complete implementation has yielded significant gains within the period, by improving the share of national employment and product in the South in the modern manufacturing sectors where state enterprise operates. In 1968 the location requirement for new plant was raised to 100 per cent, though this could be either in the South or, subject to national planning approval, in problem areas in the North or Centre regions of the country.[15] Again, it is unlikely that the Commission will be able to make much headway in extending the use of public enterprise to help Community regions if it attempts to substitute its own authority for that of the national governments. But it could play an important part in facilitating such use of public enterprise in the mobile manufacturing sector in countries such as France, Belgium, the United Kingdom and Italy which have recently introduced or extended State Holdings in manufacturing.

There also is some scope for the Commission to promote multi-national public-enterprise joint ventures in which national governments would be participants, provided the Commission tries the pragmatic role of honest broker rather than attempts to ensure that such ventures have supra-national Community status, undermining shared control by national governments of the joint venture in which they have invested public funds.

These are possibilities. But the harnessing of the location decisions of leading private and public enterprise does offer means of offsetting the asymmetry in capital and labour flows which has lain at the base of the most persistent regional inequalities in the Community to date. Basically, the control of the location of such companies need not be total. The Community would be directly confronting national governments if it tried to control the location of *all* expansions of investment over and above a given size. In this sense it would not be likely to get a Community I.D.C. policy off the ground because governments would not want to undermine such means of leverage on those national firms which can play a part in the exercise of effective economic sovereignty. But in the meso-economic league, governments have already seen some degree of sovereignty seep away at the European level, through the power of multi-national firms to threaten to locate abroad if not given the location of their choice in the national economy.

The Community might well be able to offset this degree of sovereignty 'seepage' by unanimous agreement through the Council of Ministers on a selective form of location clearance and control on British I.D.C. lines. This could be administered through a regular committee of national senior officials responsible for regional development, on the lines of the Community's Medium-Term Economic Policy Committee, which has operated 'unanimously' since 1964. Thus meso-economic, multi-national companies with turnover and employment over specified levels might be brought within a guideline system, by which they have to locate x per cent of their net increase in jobs in Community problem regions in return for selling y per cent of their sales in the Community. This could ensure that some of the most mobile and successful firms improved the competitive performance of those regions in the Community which most needed them. To prove effective this would need close co-operation between the Community and the regional planning authorities at the national level, making possible the establishment of linkages between incoming meso-economic enterprise and 'satellite' local micro-economic firms. Attention would need to be paid to ensuring that this was matched by a planned balance in the mix of industries in the regions, both within and between agriculture, manufacturing and services.

The crunch comes on the constraints which the Community and national governments might be able to employ to ensure that such guidelines were fulfilled in practice. And this brings us full circle to the role of the modern capitalist state in adjudicating between private and public interests. Multi-national companies are extremely powerful, and have shown considerable success in ensuring that national governments fulfil their corporate ends – either through lobbying or through claiming that national economic health depends on their own corporate viability. But such companies have already shown by going multi-national that they can afford the distance costs of going multi-regional. The main problem arises in the form of sanction potentially open to a nation state, or the Community, if a company tried to evade the new meso-economic location guidelines. So far only one Community economy – Italy – controls a sufficiently large and wide-ranging package of public-enterprise firms to be able to offset the multi-national challenge to its domestic market, and it was only in the late 1960s that it really began to show results in harnessing the power of multi-nationals to the development of its problem southern region. The power of the Italian State Holding Companies is both direct and indirect. Directly they can take over firms threatened by foreign multi-nationals when the latter fail to give assurances that they will expand in the South. Indirectly, they can influence multi-nationals to locate more jobs in the South through the thinly veiled threat that their subsidiaries otherwise may be taken over and incorporated into the State Holdings.

To date, the only major European parties who have advocated a major extension of public enterprise into manufacturing industry are the British Labour Party and the French Socialist and Communist parties.[16] An irony of the liberal capitalist integration of the Community to date may well be realised in the late 1970s if the member countries proceed with monetary integration without first ensuring more effective instruments for regional development. For the resulting aggravation of the problems of major regions may prompt the election to power in the most affected countries of socialist governments which choose national bases for new public enterprise and planning controls to offset regional problems caused by monetary integration.

There is, of course, an alternative if national governments and the Community cannot jointly ensure effective regional policies before 1980, capable of coping not only with the regional problem in nation states, but the problem for nation states as problem regions in the Community. If previous productivity divergences between countries continue – as is certain unless there is a major shift in the location of the most productive and efficient enterprises – national governments of either the Left or Right may either refuse to proceed with monetary integration by 1980, or declare unilateral monetary independence thereafter (to attempt the maintenance of more competitiveness through the use of exchange-rate changes). Monetary integration may prove the best formula for regional disintegration since the birth of the modern capitalist firm. Certainly the following chapter on the single-currency and federal structure of the United States shows that no reliance should be placed on harmonious self-balance through the capitalist market as a premise for regional harmony in a federal Europe.

CHAPTER 6

FEDERALISM AND THE REGIONAL PROBLEM

The previous chapters have attempted to show that the free working of the market mechanism in a capitalist system does not overcome persistent regional disparities, and that this regional imbalance is a multi-dimensional process reflecting imbalance in capitalist development rather than a purely spatial or local problem. Some of the clearest evidence on this comes from investigating the regional growth of the United States. On the other hand, U.S. regional growth was exceptional in ways which are overlooked by leading economists in the United States. As a result, the United States should not provide a model for either the federal proposals now made for the European Community nor to less-developed countries which might be encouraged to attempt to follow its lead under pressure from international institutions or the U.S. government itself. A federal structure may have helped to establish American regions, but could break countries elsewhere under different historical and regional conditions.

Self-Balance Mythology

The question whether federal integration aggravates the regional problem can be analysed in terms of the most outspoken and sophisticated argument in favour of a federal 'free-market' economy by Borts and Stein. Basing this case on the United States they also claim that their conclusions are valid for the E.E.C.[1] They take as their point of departure the free-market case of Adam Smith, and contest its challenge, in the regional context, by Gunnar Myrdal. As they write

> Our object . . . is to explain the process of growth that occurs in a free market area characterised by free trade and free

movements of productive services under conditions of full employment. Myrdal bases his conclusions concerning the effects of free capital movements upon the experiences of the developed and under-developed countries. We believe that the experiences of the component states of the United States of America are more relevant for a test of a theory of growth in a free market area than are the experiences of countries with varying degrees of political instability and different restrictions upon private enterprise.

Borts and Stein admit that Myrdal's views 'are logical, i.e. 'they contain no internal contradictions'. They also admit that it is the more rapidly growing regions which, as claimed by Myrdal, 'are likely to import capital from more slowly growing regions'. None the less, they 'adduce evidence to support the view that the rapidly growing regions have been the regions of low rather than high *per capita* income' and draw attention to the convergence trend in *per capita* incomes in the United States to claim that 'the evidence, therefore, is not compatible with Myrdal's theory of interregional differences in growth rates among open economies'.[2]

Most of Borts and Stein's analysis is critically limited by a range of unrealistic assumptions. For instance they assume (1) that the price of manufacturing products is the same for each firm regardless of its regional location; (2) that the price of capital goods to each firm in manufacturing is, on the average, the same for each firm regardless of its regional location; (3) that each manufacturing firm has the same production function, subject to constant returns to scale, and (4) that there is a limit to the size of each firm such that competition prevails and firms behave competitively. From these assumptions

the following conclusion is deduced. Inter-state differences in the rates of growth of employment in a given manufacturing industry, from one long run equilibrium to another, arise solely from inter-state differences in the rate of growth of the labour supply function. The main factor in the labour supply function is inter-state wage differentials.[3]

These assumptions undermine precisely the case which Borts and Stein claim to have proved, that is to say the claim that regional *per capita* income disparities in the United States have been reduced over given periods because of the free working of the market mechanism rather than because of government intervention. In their words, 'the model provides a picture of an open economy moving along a balanced growth path determined by the rate of growth of the labour supply'.[4] But the model not only is purely theoretical, but represents the theory of an idealised perfectly competitive capitalist system. Taking the assumptions in order they can be translated thus: (1) no interregional differentials in productivity; (2) identical capital costs for firms whatever their regional location; (3) no scale economies or cumulative scale gains to initially larger M.D.R. firms (U-shaped rather than L-shaped long-run average-cost curves and no differentials in technical progress and innovation); and (4) no dominant meso-economic or multi-national companies, and therefore no oligopolistic no-entry or elimination price tactics towards smaller-scale later-starting L.D.R. firms.

To 'test' their purely competitive model against the evidence, Borts and Stein choose to correlate returns to only the machinery sector in only one state (New England) against the rest of the United States for only the seven years between 1947 and 1954. From regression relations they conclude that

> the relative rate of growth was positively and significantly correlated with the realised rate of return. Sectors which had the highest profitabilities for expansion did, in fact, expand most rapidly. The 'invisible hand' led the regional firms in the direction of competitive equilibrium. The result is the more remarkable inasmuch as it occurred in the machinery industry, where atomistic competition is not universal.

They take these equalised rates of return to indicate that business companies throughout the United States are choosing between least-cost locations in order to maximise the marginal rates of return on investment, and that this lies behind the equalised rates and the convergence tendency in inter-state *per capita* income.[5]

The shortcomings of such a test will be obvious. On their own admission, Borts and Stein have analysed a highly oligopolistic or meso-economic industry for only one state against the rest of the national economy. The degree of meso-economic power and the extent of collusion in price fixing in the machinery sector was well illustrated by the scandal of the electrical switchgear sector at the same time as Borts and Stein were running their regressions. Four U.S. companies accounted for some 80 per cent of the national industry market for switchgear, and their executives had organised a rota system whereby each in turn gave a lower-cost bid than the others for particular contracts for generating equipment. To maintain company-division profits in line with senior management expectations, the lowest-cost bid was raised at an annual percentage rate above the average for industry as a whole. It was only by chance that the Federal Bureau of Investigation broke this joint monopoly price ring, after months of initially fruitless work, with the result that several company executives briefly went to gaol.[6] The degree of comparable collusion throughout the rest of the U.S. machinery sector cannot be proved by running regressions of the Borts and Stein type as a counter to their case. Certainly the F.B.I.'s wire-tapping facilities are not open to the present author. But it is clear that what Borts and Stein almost certainly are measuring in the machinery case is not the entrepreneurial maximisation of least-cost locations, but meso-economic profits in a highly concentrated sector where indivisibilities and capital costs mean no-entry barriers in addition to any other pricing tactics which national leader firms may employ to deter entry or eliminate regional challengers. Apart from which, the association of highest growth with highest profit opportunities is an interesting indication of the continued responsiveness of capitalist management to profit – especially where their own price collusion may ensure a smooth and high profits path facilitating the spreading of high fixed costs. It is *not* an indication of the competitive price and location assumptions on which Borts and Stein base their model.[7]

Bort and Stein therefore assume away the barriers from oligopoly and meso-economic power which constitute one of the main reasons why later-starting L.D.R. firms will find it difficult or impossible to penetrate M.D.R. and main national markets.

They thereby avoid the evidence that leading U.S. national companies have been going multi-national rather than multi-regional – locating more investment and employment abroad than in Appalachia or the Deep South. Their assumption of perfectly competitive, cost-minimising location behaviour has also avoided the industry-mix problem in the problem regions of the United States by taking only a one-industry two-region model (New England versus the rest of the United States). *If* capitalist firms in the United States behaved as their model of federal growth assumes, both intra-industry and inter-industry regional shares would conform with the national pattern in the footloose manufacturing sector (rather than location-tied industries such as mining). But analysis shows that the machinery sector studied by Borts and Stein was significantly under-represented in the main problem region of the United States (the South rather than New England) in 1960 (four years before the publication of the Borts and Stein study). As a Twentieth Century Fund study concluded,

electrical machinery, the metal industry, transportation equipment and non-electrical manufacturing machinery ... in general are high-wage, capital-intensive industries that could make important contributions to improving the South's wage structure and income distribution. It is significant, however, that in 1960 in the South these four manufacturing industries accounted for only 39 per cent of the increased employment in twelve above-average-growth manufacturing industries, compared to 58 per cent for the nation as a whole, and that only about 5 per cent of the South's total employment was in these four industries, compared to about 12 per cent in the nation. The manufacturing industries that had the greatest increases in employment in the South between 1940 and 1960 were the traditionally low-wage, labour-intensive apparel and food processing industries that use a high proportion of unskilled labour.[8]

The Borts and Stein case that the Myrdal thesis is refuted on the basis of their findings on *per capita* income and growth is even weaker, and is undermined by their own evidence. For instance, they derive two testable hypotheses from their perfect competition theory:

(1) that low-wage regions will experience the highest rates of growth of capital and of the capital–labour ratio;

(2) that low-wage regions will experience the highest rates of growth of wages.

These hypotheses were studied for three periods: 1919–29, 1929–48, and 1948–53. As they themselves admit, 'the explanatory power of the aggregative model is quite weak. In the first and third periods capital grew at a greater rate in the high-wage areas than in the low wage areas. Moreover, the wage grew faster in the high-wage areas during the same periods. Employment grew perceptibly more rapidly in the high-wage areas only during the middle period.' One can agree, without difficulty, their conclusion that 'the theory is refuted for the periods 1919–29 and 1948–53 but is compatible with the data during the 1929–48 period'.[9] What is more difficult to accept is why a 'once-up and twice-down' result should persuade one to hold on to the theory, particularly when it is alleged to be the evidence on which refutation of the Myrdal case is based.

It also is striking that their 'empirically based' theory claims that 'the major factors which influence the businessman's choice of the location of investment are the marginal rates of return which have occurred in the various possible geographical areas in which investments have been made', yet they produce no empirical evidence whatsoever to support the claim. A similar empirical lapse occurs in their argument in terms of neglect of the spatial inelasticity of labour migration – the less migration the further the move. It is this rather than their, in itself, banal observation that some labour moves from low- to high-wage areas which underlies the labour-migration problem, just as the inertia of management and the preference for expansion on or near initial sites underlies the failure of sufficient capital to migrate to the labour-outflow areas to reduce interregional and national income disparities on the lines claimed by the model. The same neglect of available evidence on the urban unemployment of immigrants to city core areas and the link between the northern urban crisis and emigration from southern problem regions undermines the 'success story' theme in their analysis of the role of the 'labour-supply function' in U.S. federal growth.[10]

Unique Factors in U.S. Regional Growth

There are many reasons why the U.S. federal integration case should not be exported to the E.E.C. as a model for the automatic convergence of lagging with leading regions through the free working of the market mechanism in a single-currency area. They include the theoretical analysis of previous chapters which has indicated that labour migration under free-market conditions will raise the full-employment ceiling of labour-inflow areas without depleting the unemployment pool of less-developed regions; the cumulative stimulus to capital accumulation and inflow from raised expectations of profits through sustained growth in the capital-and labour-inflow region; the intra-sectoral backwash effects of faster innovating, meso-economic M.D.R. firms on slower-growing, micro-economic L.D.R. competitors; the no-entry and elimination pricing effects from either destabilised or stable prices held by national leaders during a period of rising costs for themselves and their L.D.R. challengers; the tendency to multi-national rather than multi-regional location by leading M.D.R. firms; the inertia of medium-and small-sized firms when faced with the possibility of a new plant in an L.D.R. location, and the variety of further previously analysed factors which tend to reinforce dualistic markets and supply structures in problem regions. These general factors should be borne in mind as background to the specific criticisms of the free-market convergence case, as should the claim that it is mainly because of government intervention – however limited in its effects – that minor convergence tendencies have been registered in some integrated economies such as the E.E.C.

But in the U.S. case there are also at least a dozen particular reasons why there has been a trend to regional convergence in *per capita* income, including both unique historical factors and the role of state and local governments through the nineteenth and twentieth centuries. Both their uniqueness and their scale further undermine the free-market case apart from its challenge by Myrdalian and neo-Marxist cumulative disequilibrium theory.

(1) The U.S. capitalist economy grew from exploitation of a new and effectively virgin colony rather than the integration of

already developed and competitive industrial regions, or the integration of efficient capitalist farming with inefficient peasant agriculture. One result was free or very cheap land and natural resources. The new colonialists therefore did not have to pay Ricardian rent, enjoying a very low real cost for land and resource exploitation. This meant a production advantage relative to agricultural producers in the Old World capitalist economies which was to be sustained through the nineteenth century for many producers and farmers as the frontier of the still developing country rolled westwards. When the advantage was later lost, particularly for many second-generation capitalist farmers who had to meet rising mortgage indebtedness and increasing world competition, the more familiar backwash effects reasserted themselves.

(2) The new colonial population consisted mainly of the more enterprising and gain-orientated emigrants from the Old World. The coincidence of early immigration with the Protestant Ethic, and its role in the foundation of U.S. capitalism has been open to question. But, in general, it seems clear that whatever the mechanism of cause and effect involved, both entrepreneurs and workers in the colonial period showed a higher degree of motivation than either the feudal landlords of Latin America or the neo-feudal or caste-dominated economies of many less-developed countries today. Certainly religion was not a sufficient factor. God helped those who were on good terms with the colonial administration, and the administrators helped themselves. But, in general, the whole of the U.S. economy was to become an inflow region for European capital and labour. It thereby gained Myrdalian 'spread' effects on a major scale, while the 'backwashed' areas were those in Europe depleted of both capital and their more skilled labour. There were two main dimensions to the process: (i) the 'push' effect of the new capitalist entrepreneurs, able and willing to exploit the new free resources; and (ii) the 'pull' effect on the new immigrant workers from abroad (mainly Ireland and the South of Italy) who were attracted both by the employment and income opportunities in existing enterprise, and the chance of becoming self-employed farmers and handicraft workers. Moreover, immigration only began to rise at a substantial rate from 1840 onwards, when the demand for labour in the

industrialising economy of the North-East was accompanied by the Great Famine in Ireland – a unique disaster which overcame more normal labour resistance to migration.[11]

(3) The southern and south-eastern states benefited from a comparative advantage in the production of three commodities – sugar, cotton and tobacco – which had no sizeable sources of alternative supply in either Europe or the main industrialising region of the economy, the North-East. This had two self-reinforcing effects. First, it helped sustain an export-based growth in the South, and secondly a reverse export flow for the North-East's manufactures, giving the latter area a high income interregional trade during a period in which industrial trade in the international economy was dominated by Britain.[12] This complementarity depended upon the comparative advantage of the South in agricultural products (a complementarity later to be matched by the Plains and the Mid-West in grains and beef) which would not have been possible in industrial integration if the South had produced goods in which it had to compete with the rest of the country on the basis of absolute advantage or disadvantage.

(4) Even more uniquely, the southern farmers of the pre-Civil War period were able to exploit slave labour at literally subsistence cost, permitting them to earn super-normal profit levels and generate higher regional capital by the simple expedient of not paying any wages at all. Despite the fact that the southern regional economy was later 'backwashed' by the rising industrial economy of the North and despite its incapacity for social and economic reasons to adapt its specialisation to new indigenous manufacturing, the slave-labour economy was crucial in permitting a sustained breakthrough on a once-and-for-all basis to an export economy with a large surplus and high consequential expenditure for a minority ruling class. The southern states also benefited from low-cost labour after the Civil War, when constitutional freedoms for blacks were not matched by inter-racial income equalisation in the region.

(5) The north-eastern seaboard states in the United States were the first to employ capital-intensive techniques of production and invention which had hitherto not been employed in the European countries (especially Britain) where they had been invented. The reasons related to the kind of mechanism which

have previously been described in the dynamics of capital
accumulation in a labour-inflow region which is approaching an
indigenous full-employment ceiling. Basically, the flow of
immigrants to the United States helped raise the full-
employment ceiling of the north-eastern industrial economy in
the mid-nineteenth century by making available a continual
stream of new labour which restrained the wage–cost spiral.
Simultaneously European capital – especially British capital –
was attracted to the fast-developing new industrial economy.
But while the sustained inflow of both factors of production
maintained entrepreneurial confidence in long-term growth of
profits, some of the immigrants were not attracted to industry at
all, but to farming on low-cost land. Therefore there was a
labour shortage (relative to Europe) under high macro-
economic growth conditions, encouraging more capital-
intensive and innovation-embodying techniques of production
as well as higher wages.[13] This would not have been possible in an
already heavily populated economy with a large agricultural
working population such as most of the less-developed countries
to which U.S. models of capital accumulation are currently being
exported by aid and development agencies.

(6) The initial growth of the U.S. north-eastern seaboard
economy was undertaken on classic protectionist rather than on
international *laissez-faire* lines. The U.S. government may now
advocate liberalisation of trade between itself and less-developed
countries, much as the West German authorities are now the
most ardent liberalisation advocates in the E.E.C. But, like the
economy of the German Reich, the U.S. industrial economy
grew behind some of the most substantial and progressively
rising industrial tariffs ever imposed – from the initial tariff in
1796, and raised tariffs in 1816 and 1828. In regional terms the
North-east economy of the United States avoided the import-led
decline of the von Neumann Whitman type by reducing imports
and promoting import-substitution, while at the same time
welcoming the capital and labour inflow from abroad which
helped finance innovation and prevented a regional labour
bottleneck. In fact, it was his personal experience of the results
of such tariff protection which encouraged Friedrich List to
make his challenge to the 'classical growth through liberalisation' case and express the first 'infant industries' protection

argument, which was adopted by his friends in the German Zollverein, and later by Bismarck in introducing major industrial tariffs in the Reich.[14]

(7) While the regional industrial economy of the North-East of the United States grew behind such protection against European imports, the pre-railway cost of transport for industrial goods and the only gradually emerging pattern of large-scale production meant that the other developing regions of the United States – including that part of the South which was not rapidly reached by sea and inland water transport – was *distance*-protected rather than tariff-protected.[15] This is a condition which does not now obtain for the manufacturing and consumer goods industries of the main regional centres in less-developed countries, and a condition which is actually *undermined* by the road building programme and infrastructural improvements undertaken by most governments in developed economies if they also directly assist infant firms and industries in the regions. In other words, distance protection in the early and mid-nineteenth century in the United States ensured that local entrepreneurs could supply local manufacturing markets, and thereby generate both savings for further capital accumulation and income multipliers which had low leakages from the locality or region. They could do this despite the fact that they were initially less competitive in cost terms than their north-eastern counterparts who were not yet effective national competitors.[16]

(8) The availability of an efficient railway technology by the mid-nineteenth century made possible the construction of national low-cost, distance-shrinking communications. The grain and livestock market of the central farming areas of the Mid-West – like the cotton and tobacco market of the South – was complementary rather than competitive with the industrial markets of the North-East and the newly expanding Great Lakes industrial area. In other words, it was different from the interregional industrial trade of some of the principal problem regions in the E.E.C., which neither have a comparative advantage in agricultural production (South Italy and West France versus the Lombardy plain and the Beauce wheat plain), nor have an absolute advantage in industrial production towards their M.D.R. national and international competitors.[17]

(9) Unlike peasant agriculture in heavily populated problem

regions in both developed and underdeveloped capitalist economies, the capitalist agriculture of the U.S. Mid-West and Far West enjoyed the cumulative and now unrepeatable advantages of (i) free land under the Homestead Acts with indirect effects on low resale prices; (ii) high land–labour ratios for the period that such free land was available; (iii) an 'optimisation' of land–labour ratios in the sense of the newly arrived settler finding by experience what was the maximum territory he could exploit with his given labour force; (iv) super-normal profits and fast capital accumulation both from the free-land and cheap-land policies, and from the windfall gains to be made during the period in which the industrial regions' demand for meat only gradually adjusted to the lower prices which railway transportation permitted; (v) a major surplus in excess of the demand of the industrialised eastern and north-central regions which the railways and, later, steam sea transport could market in Western Europe, which was still handicapped by a predominantly peasant agriculture; (vi) an inflow of foreign as well as industrial regions' capital to benefit from the super-normal profits to be made, permitting the retention of regional savings for further agricultural and non-agricultural development; (vii) new social infrastructure and services of a kind which could benefit later local industry in some of the key farming states, as well as (viii) new local and non-local demand for agricultural machinery.[18]

(10) Like Mid-West U.S. agriculture, the railroad expansion which permitted the complementary linkage of mainly industrial and mainly agricultural regions, plus the export of agriculture to Europe, was substantially financed by foreign rather than regional or interregional U.S. capital. This came mainly from European financiers who either had seen the peak of their own railroad boom or could earn less in further European railroad development than in the United States. Again unique factors reinforced the U.S. railroad rush, which registered a 300 per cent employment increase from 1840 to 1860 against a 100 per cent increase in Britain. First, railways were virtually in a monopsonistic position in providing eastwards transport for the agriculture of the central plains. In Western Europe they had to compete with an already relatively developed road and canal network.[19] Secondly, the railway companies not only were

given free land on which to construct track – unlike European companies – but also were given vast tracts of land in the areas which they developed as an incentive to development. Thirdly, this not only meant higher profits than were possible in Western Europe, but also meant that the railway companies diversified from the start into property development and leasing, local banking and finance and other services sectors, raising the profit level of the companies and their attraction to foreign capital in an unparalleled manner. These direct multiplier effects on the regional economies in which the railways operated were supplementary to the indirect multipliers of consequential investment and employment expenditure, and the externalities which the railways permitted.[20]

(11) Virtually all the U.S. states had some exceptional resource-endowment advantage. In Roman times Sicily and the South of Italy were the grain and timber yards of the Empire, but their exploitation over centuries has left them basically depleted. In the United States the late development of the Pacific North-West and of California meant that two of the most peripheral areas in the country were opened up in virtually virgin condition at a time when the industrialised eastern regions needed greater quantities of not only the old resource of timber, but also the newly discovered resource of mineral oil for fuel consumption. The same new demand for oil benefited Texas landowners who were beginning to suffer from declining relative productivity in cattle raising. In the peripheral state of Florida natural climate advantages permitted not merely recreational services, but also significant retirement colonies of the monied middle class, which gave a permanent non-cyclical demand for goods and services. In California climate also attracted the development of the world's main cinema industry during the boom period for the cinema of the 1920s and 1930s. In both states, the Miami Beach and Hollywood images perpetuated the pull of retirement and speculative incomes, with the retired and the super-rich injecting incomes into the local economy without making a direct claim on local employment. In other words, the rise of a modern services structure not only sustained economic growth in the system at a national level, but was secured in regionally dispersed services growth poles – in different regions from the original mining, forestry

and manufacturing regions. Sectoral advance, therefore, was accompanied by spatial-regional spread in a fortuitous manner (climate rather than endogenous self-adjustment through free market growth), much as the historical development of the administrative capitals of the Electorates in Germany provided growth centres of a kind from which the present West German federal and Länder authorities are now benefiting.

(12) While these factors were all on the credit side for U.S. regional growth, a variety of further factors ensured that, up to the Civil War, the national economy did not grow at the cost of significant Myrdal-type backwash effects in its constituent regions. The inflow of foreign capital and labour into agriculture and mining occurred simultaneously with the development of modern industry, so that the U.S. economy missed the first stage of the Rostow growth theory (the pre-condition of generating an agricultural surplus for investment in industry). In Rostow terms it gained both stages one and two at one immigrant bound.[21] In Lutz terms, the inflow of foreign capital to both industry and agriculture meant that most of the agricultural surplus could be retained for modernisation of capitalist agriculture (as opposed to being drained by peasant agriculture), while the remainder could be profitably employed in modern industry rather than in backwashed local industry.[22] Also, the fact that labour and capital inflow came from abroad rather than from the working population in agriculture or declining industries meant that each successively exploited region in the United States constituted a more-developed region in relation to the foreign factor-outflow regions. Consequently each region benefited from a raised full-employment ceiling, high natural and warranted growth, and an export-led growth component without (i) depleting the investible capital or selectively undermining the labour force of other national regions, (ii) reducing their natural and warranted growth rates, or (iii) their export-led growth potential. There clearly were interregional capital and migration flows, but where there were they tended to be of the overflow rather than the syphoning variety for capital, with throughflow rather than overflow for labour. In other words, the U.S. economy *as a whole* was the world's fastest developing factor-inflow region through the nineteenth century, with unequal but high 'spread' gains for

most regions, and with few or negligible 'backwash' effects on national regions rather than international regions elsewhere.

Comparison with International Integration Theory

The uniqueness of the U.S. case and the extent to which it is therefore undermined as a model of self-adjusting regional growth can be summarised in relation to the international integration theory spelled out earlier in the text. The U.S. national economy up to the Civil War appears to have benefited from all of the five main factors in the liberalist case for international integration: (1) stimulated competition; (2) specialisation in production; (3) scale economies in production and distribution; (4) high productivity and fast output growth, and (5) competitive strength in foreign markets. But it did so with several important differences.

(1) the competition was behind a prohibitive national tariff, with initial competition between equally infant industries, rather than their exposure through 'integration' in a free-trade area with an unequal competitor, which could have resulted in a high rate of infant-firm mortalities;

(2) the specialisation in production was in agricultural products and raw materials in which the country had a natural comparative advantage (cotton, tobacco, wheat, livestock and, later, oil) as well as manufacturing products, while regional specialisation was mainly complementary rather than competitive, between agricultural, mining, forestry and, later, oil-exploiting regions on the one hand and manufacturing regions on the other;

(3) the scale economies in production and distribution were stimulated by a large internal market (one of the factors which most impressed List) but this stimulation was initially within distance-protected markets which nurtured the growth of spatially distributed and large-scale enterprise, capable of multi-product and conglomerate diversification as their regional markets became gradually integrated through rail transport;

(4) high productivity and a fast rate of growth of output was stimulated not by integration of previous markets in which specialisation and productivity gains had not been possible because of lack of a sufficient 'home market', but by (i) increased

capital intensity and innovation because of relative labour shortage, and (ii) a complementary fast growth of population exploiting free or cheap land and raw material resources, with both made possible by factor immigration into the national economy rather than simply interregional migration within it;

(5) the competitive strength of the U.S. economy depended on such factors rather than the inter-penetration of previous regional markets into a national economy, with the benefits of a massive domestic market under-pinning the pyramid of a diversified regional structure part of which – like the pyramids themselves – had been established with slave labour.

The bonanza could not and did not last. From the late 1860s the self-adjustment of new regions complementing already fast developing older regions ran into trouble as the variety of unique factors on which that self-adjustment had been based gave way to the variety of cumulative self-imbalancing factors observable in the longer-run growth of capitalist systems. This showed clearly in the plight of the small-scale capitalist farmer and the rising agrarian discontent expressed in the Granger movement, the Greenback movement and later in the rise of the Populists. The factors can be summarised thus:

(1) The free land in new regions progressively ran out as the expanding federation spread its upper and lower geographical limits along the Canadian and Mexican borders and reached the Pacific.

(2) The increasing cost of land was reflected in the high percentage of mortgages held by second-generation capitalist smallholders, with mortgaged properties accounting for 40 per cent of the total number of holdings in the North-Central region as late as 1890, with proportions as high as 54 per cent in Nebraska and 60 per cent in Kansas.[23]

(3) The increased dependence of farmers on world agricultural markets heightened their dependence on cyclical variations in those markets. The farmer 'found himself competing in a world market in which the fluctuations in prices made no apparent sense to him. The bottom might drop out of his income because of a bumper crop on the other side of the world.'[24]

(4) The traditional difficulties of modernising capitalist agriculture could not be met by many capitalist smallholders

under conditions of mortgage indebtedness and market fluctuations. As debt payments to the banks and conglomerates could not be met, many such farmers were forced into involuntary migration with their families.

(5) Over-all agricultural productivity in the United States did not significantly recover until after the 1929 Depression and the New Deal policies (aimed at 'getting the farmer out of the mud'); even marked labour outflow from small-scale farming was offset by the natural increase in agricultural working population in those families which could afford to stay in farming but could not afford to find jobs elsewhere.[25]

In industry and services the increasing integration of the national market from the 1860s onwards gave rise to new problems. Again, these can be cross-referred to the main features of the liberalist case for international integration.

(1) The 'demand pull' of the national markets now opened through transport advances was accompanied by a second-generation 'technology push' as new products and services became available (steel substituted for iron; the development and application of electricity to industrial and consumer power needs; the development of the electrical household appliances industry; the substitution of gas for kerosene; and finally the exploitation of refined petroleum for the newly developed internal-combustion engine).

(2) The scale economies made possible through new technical processes, and the necessity of ensuring such scale to survive the competition of other larger-scale producers and distributors, gave rise to heightened risks in the production and distribution of the new goods and services. The high productivity gains from specialisation and scale economies were put at risk by precisely the increased competition in a distance-integrated market which is one of the allegedly complementary characteristics of the liberalist integration case.

(3) The result of the dual pincer effect of increased risk and lowered profits through increased competition was the rise from the 1880s of collusive trusts on a scale never before experienced in world capitalist development. The trust brought the control of a number of leading firms into the hands of a single board of directors on which each 'competitor' was represented, eliminat-

ing the competition problem for those large and fortunate enough to be represented in the first place.

(4) The regional result was a process of national integration for the new industries and services which operated largely through the rate and pace with which the trusts shared out regional markets between themselves and consumed or eliminated regional competitors. For some time few constraints were observed in this process, although it later became appreciated that permitting higher-cost smaller and localised competitors to survive was both good public relations and increased the profit margin for leading firms with lower costs.

(5) The national political result of the trusts was the introduction of the Sherman Anti-Trust Act in 1890 which formally outlawed trusts and made other informal monopolistic practices illegal. But it was fourteen years until the first major successful case was won under the legislation (against the Harriman-Morgan Northern Securities combine), and since 1911 when the courts ordered the break up of the Standard Oil and American Tobacco companies into *regionalised* and competitive concerns, the leading companies have learned (i) to act more circumspectly in domestic-market sharing and (ii) to go *multinational* rather than *multi-regional* in order to escape the trust busters. No major company was broken up over the next seventy-five years.[26]

On the labour supply and migration front, the high Italian immigration of the later nineteenth century and the pre-First World War period had sustained the raised full-employment ceiling effect for the U.S. economy as a whole following the fall-off in Irish immigration rates after the Great Famine. But several factors changed the international immigration picture into the interregional migration problem with which capitalist economies elsewhere have been largely unable to cope.

(1) The reduction of European immigration during the 1914–18 period was accompanied by an increased demand for labour in the industrial areas of the North-East through the demand for armaments and through the labour-depletion effect of recruitment when the United States joined the war.

(2) This labour vacuum was filled on a major scale for the first time by black immigrants from the South.

(3) The recovery of higher immigration and the return of

soldiers to peacetime employment reduced the initial rate of immigration from the South but the war had broken the threshold which had previously restrained large-scale black immigration.

(4) The war thereby broke down the race and inertia barriers to major labour migration between the least- and most-developed U.S. regions much as the railway transport revolution had broken the distance protection of interregional product markets and trade.

(5) The 'follow-the-leader' effects of the settlement of some black families in ghetto conditions in the North-East was insufficient to reduce total population in the South but sufficient to begin the vicious circle of age and skill depletion for the areas of labour outflow and the slum-unemployment syndrome in the main inflow city core areas, especially as the natural rate of increase of the new ghetto dwellers was higher than that of the white communities which they replaced.

In other words, the interregional backwash effects of labour migration had begun to be registered from the end of the Civil War in agriculture, industry, services and agriculture, offsetting the spread effects from the growth of the national economy up to 1929.

State Capitalism and U.S. Regional Growth

It has been seen that Borts and Stein claim that 'the experience of the component states of the United States of America are more relevant for a test of the theory of growth in a free market area than are the experiences of countries with varying degrees of political instability and different restrictions upon private enterprises'.[27] But political stability and a particular set of anti-trust restrictions on private-enterprise freedom do not amount to a free market economy, and in claiming that they do Borts and Stein are only presenting part of the picture. Research over the last seventy years has shown that the claim that U.S. regional economic growth represented the flowering of a virginal, unadulterated private capitalism is a myth. The evidence is worth assembling as a counterbalance to the free-market regional self-balance mythology. It is also interesting because of the extent of state capitalist enterprise which it reveals in early U.S. regional growth, which has its own implications for public enterprise as a regional development instrument in the late twentieth century.

It has already been seen that the government of the newly independent United States immediately pressed and extended a policy of rigorous protection to create a sufficient home market for the development of infant firms and industries. This was hardly the first case of political intervention in the free working of the market. In the colonial period, as Kolko has put it, the capitalist entrepreneurship of the Protestant Ethic was even less significant than 'a political capitalism in which economic success was determined far more by political and social connections than by any special religious motivations'.[28] The origins of this situation have been traced by Bailyn to the determination of the British government of the Restoration period to secure a closer supervision of the administration of the Empire through the granting of government contracts, for tax collection, customs regulation and bestowal of land grants, to a chosen 'inner circle'. Bailyn chronicles the accumulation of New England fortunes through such inner-circle means, and points to an initial accumulation of capital which had little to do with self-adjustment models of primitive accumulation of an agricultural surplus later to be invested in industry.[29]

Bruchey has also shown that, in the immediate post-independence period, 'given the strength of the American desire for economic development, the scarcity of capital funds and the sharpness of competition from foreign suppliers, manufacturing was endowed with a quasi-public and not a private character, and given numerous encouragements by the State'. The main mechanism of this public intervention com-pared directly with the use of state shareholding in public companies in Italy and France from the 1930s onwards – incorporation of the business enterprise as a state agency to fulfil public rather than merely private ends. Bruchey points out that during the colonial period incorporation had been em-ployed only about half-a-dozen times for business organisations. But, in contrast, state governments created more than three hundred business corporations between the end of the Revolu-tion and 1801. Two-thirds of them were to establish inland navigation, toll bridges and turnpike roads. Thirty-two companies were initiated in insurance to underwrite risks which private enterprise would not take, thirty-four in banking, and thirty-six in water resource projects and dock building.[30]

But this state supplementation of the 'invisible hand' was only a foretaste of greater things to come. Some seventy years ago Guy Callender had already challenged the private-enterprise mythology of U.S. economic development with an analysis which Borts and Stein have wisely chosen to neglect. As he wrote in 1902,

> it is a commonplace observation that the last century witnessed everywhere a great extension of the activities of the State into the field of industry. Americans are not accustomed to think of their own country as taking a prominent part in this movement, far less as ever having occupied a leading position in it. To them, as to the rest of the world, America is the land of private enterprise *par excellence*; the place where 'State interference' has played the smallest part, and individual enterprise has been given the largest scope, in industrial affairs; and it is commonly assumed that this has always been so. Nevertheless it is a fact that this country was one of the first to exhibit this modern tendency to extend the activity of the State into industry.[31]

Callender showed that government intervention in the economy was not simply a post-Independence accident, but the precondition and continuing accompaniment of the opening of the major regional economy of the Mid-West, and of the subsequent inflow of private capital to that region which has already been described. State governments, with federal blessing and federal participation, opened up the transport links which pierced the Appalachian barrier and created the conditions under which new emigrants to the Mid-West could export from that region to the Eastern seaboard. As Callender says,

> up to 1815 the improvements of rivers and building of canals, which alone could enable remote regions to send their produce to market, had been almost entirely neglected. Numerous efforts had been made to induce capital to take up this work, but with very little success.... In the settlement of

the West and the development of its resources, men were even less inclined to risk their capital. I have found no evidence that any Eastern capital was invested in this way before 1815. The settler moved into the wilderness with his own little stock of household goods, farm implements and cattle. No merchant with large credit in the East stood ready to advance supplies of food and other necessaries to him, nor was he assisted to clear his land and prepare it for cultivation by loans of cash from individuals or mortgage companies. Of course there were banks in the new States, but most of them were mere paper money machines with no real capital at all, and those that had a real instead of a nominal capital had to depend more upon local than upon Eastern supplies.[32]

It was intervention by the states which transformed this situation. New York led the way with the Erie canal in 1817, and Pennsylvania followed in 1825 with an equally extensive system of canals; Maryland, Virginia and the federal government began the Chesapeake and Ohio canal in 1828, and Virginia pushed through an earlier project to connect the James river with the Ohio from 1820 onwards. Railway projects were pioneered by the states – the Baltimore and Ohio in 1828; the Erie in New York in the early 1830s, with subsequent developments of state-financed railways and canals in Indiana, Michigan and Illinois. It was this breakthrough in railway construction through state finance that attracted foreign capital to follow up. In the words of Callender

to construct these important projects required several millions of capital – an amount far greater than had been brought together in any industry at that time. For corporations to secure so much capital it was necessary to bring together the small savings of the country and to attract the large ones of foreigners. There was no body of private individuals in the country well enough known and with sufficient influence in the business world to establish the credit of a corporation so that it could command the confidence of both these classes of investors. The only securities that could do so were public securities, or the securities of corporations which were guaranteed or assisted by the government.... When New York demonstrated that it was easy to secure all the capital necessary for carrying out public works by the issue of bonds on the credit of the State, the way was open for other States to pursue the same course, and only New Jersey and the smaller New England States refused to enter upon it.[33]

The role of the federal government was less important in these state capitalist developments than that of the states themselves, and federal expenditure anyway declined temporarily before the Civil War, as the southern states increasingly opposed federal intervention. However, according to Davis and Legler, federal expenditure approximately equalled the states' expenditure throughout the nineteenth century. Military expenditure accounted for nearly 40 per cent of the federal total from 1815 to 1902, administrative expenses for about half, and public works for the remainder. In general, they claim that federal policy was 'designed to grab whatever was at hand to pay the bills for expenditures dictated by the political process'. None the less, federal expenditure had fiscal transfer effects, and 'because there were regional differences in expenditures and receipts, these effects had a spatial dimension'.[34]

The regional-aid effects of this federal expenditure were massive by any twentieth-century standards, and assured income transfers to some of the main under-developed and incipient problem regions of the country long before the New Deal. For instance, the Old South was a regular and substantial deficit region, with the reverse income transfer in its favour increasing as federal expenditure increased. This arose partly from the fact that Baltimore was the only major international port in the region, partly from its inclusion of Washington D.C., and partly because of the increased political responsibility for the South after the Civil War. But the result was a deficit (or federal transfer in the region's favour) reaching nine dollars *per capita* in 1900, or one dollar for every eight of the region's income. The Mountain states' benefits from federal expenditure were even more marked. With more or less free land after 1863 and a high level of expenditure on Indian and Mormon pacification (40 per cent of the federal total in 1880) they averaged a deficit of twelve dollars *per capita* over the last quarter of the century reaching a peak of 45 dollars *per capita*, or one dollar in four of income, in 1870. The East-North-Central and East-South-Central regions were major surplus areas in federal receipts through the century, largely as a result of revenues from federal land sales. On the other hand, their benefit from the Homestead Act prevented them from subsidising the rest of the nation in real terms. Moreover, as Davis and Legler comment, 'although the Indians were something of a problem in the West, it is inconceivable that they could have done enough damage to offset the military expenditures incurred in pacifying them'.[35]

A federal budget proper, rather than taking what was available for what was regionally necessary, did not emerge until 1921. Also, planned federal intervention in favour of depressed and problem regions did not emerge in the United States until after 1929 and the Democratic New Deal. Two of its most important dimensions were (1) the general infrastructure expenditure programme on roads, and (2) selective infrastructure projects on water-resource power and control systems, of which the Tennessee Valley Authority and major dam projects are the most notable and best-known examples. Granted the scale and nature of government intervention in infrastructure and water-resource projects up to 150 years earlier it might well appear that the New Deal was an Old Deal resurrected. Even the cost–benefit analysis which stemmed in large part from the Tennessee Valley project and has since been heralded as a regional science 'discovery' had been employed as a justification for government regional development expenditure in congressional debates in 1818, when Clay argued in relation to water and road projects that

> the capitalist who should invest his money in these projects might not be reimbursed 3 per cent annually, and yet society in various forms might actually reap 15 or 20 per cent. The benefit resulting from a turnpike road made by private associations is divided between the capitalist, who receives his toll, the lands through which it passes and which are augmented in their value, and the commodities whose value is enhanced by their diminished expense of transportation.[36]

It was as a result of such a divergence between private and social benefits that Clay and others promoted direct government expenditure projects to open up inaccessible regions, promote markets and sustain growth.

One of the problems faced by the twentieth-century New Dealers was the hold which market mythology and market concentration had simultaneously exercised in the United States. The post-1929 depression had followed a period of unprecedented dynamism in the distribution of new products, techniques and facilities in entirely new industries and services. The concept of the federal government intervening directly in the market with its own enterprise in order to channel expenditure into problem regions and areas was almost inconceivable in an economy with the most developed and sophisticated capitalist companies in the world. The blame for the under-employment of resources in particular regions was also obscured by the national problem of unemployment. The demand-orientated Keynesian policies which might secure a fuller utilisation of existing capacity would neither secure a major increase in the supply of branch plants of leading companies in problem regions, nor lead to newly flowering indigenous regional enterprise capable of holding its own with the world's leading companies in national markets.

CHAPTER 7

STRATEGY FOR REGIONAL
DEVELOPMENT

New policy imperatives for regional development amount essentially to re-establishing the firm and enterprise at the centre of regional strategy itself. The previous analysis has shown that, while macro-economic theory and policy has an important role to play, it is increasingly eroded by the power of meso-economic enterprise. At this level, the key to the regional problem lies not with the regional firm, but with the national and multi-national firm. The inequality of modern capitalist competition strengthens the strong firm at the expense of the weak. There are exceptions to this rule, but they are of diminishing importance with the accelerating trend to monopoly capital in Western Europe, and the multi-nationalisation of both U.S. and European capital around the world. Any regional policy neglecting these factors is doomed to continue the disappointments and false hopes experienced in post-war development policy in most of the liberal capitalist countries.

Harnessing Meso-Economic Power

Most of the previous chapters have indicated the importance of controlling the location of leading firms. To offset the regional inequality which in practice is a spatial dimension of competitive inequality, the growth potential of leading firms must be harnessed in the interest of problem regions. If the real world conformed with the self-adjusting-migration assumptions of neo-classical theory, labour would move on a sufficient scale to where the leading firms choose to locate; congestion costs would act as a disincentive to the continuous expansion of leading firms in more-developed regions, and the need for labour would ensure that any insufficiency of labour immigration was offset by capital emigration to problem regions. But, in practice, labour does not move on a sufficient scale to equalise interregional income and employment levels; firms do not pay the full burden of congestion costs in more-developed areas; rising capital intensity, or the substitution of capital for labour, ensures that manufacturing firms can secure most of their diminishing labour requirements over the long term through immigration; also, when they take advantage of abundant and low-cost labour, the national leaders tend to do so by going multi-national to labour havens in the Third World; combined with the transfer pricing available through their multi-national operations, this tends to mean economic gains far in excess of regional disincentives such as congestion taxes or government regional incentives in favour of national problem regions. It is therefore imperative for governments in the mature capitalist economies to find means of harnessing the location of such firms if they wish to ensure any radical improvement in the condition and prospects of their problem regions.

There are three main criteria for the distinction of firms in regional policy: (1) 'leader' firms; (2) 'led' firms; and (3) 'laggard' firms. Basically, leader firms are those companies which are the pace-setters in national and international capitalist growth. They are generally meso-economic, multi-national and independent in corporate policy – product innovation, market penetration, access to finance, sales, distribution and location. The second category, led firms, are dependent for the main part on national markets and exports (rather than multi-national production and sales). They therefore fall more into the micro-economic sphere where domestic Keynesian policies are effective. But, in general, they are not sufficiently large to be able to pose a competitive challenge to the meso-economic, multi-national leaders. They either wait for their lead in innovation or market development, or seek to operate in a satellite function relative to the leaders (providing quality bulk inputs over the long term; sub-contracting for the leaders, and so on). The third category, laggard firms, constitutes the rest of the national market. They are too small to bother the leaders, or to prove attractive to them as providers of inputs or as sub-contractors. They survive under the 'price umbrella' offered by leader firms, choose in general against price competition, and tend to be local or regional concerns posing little threat in national markets.

The evolution of specific criteria for such different types of firm would vary from one economy to another. Because the distinctions are mainly qualitative, they will not conform simply with differences in size. Size alone is neither an index of multi-national activity, nor an indication of leadership relatively to smaller firms in areas such as innovation, price, transfer pricing, and so on. By the same token, meso-economic concerns which have a significant impact on macro-economic performance (such as state monopolies in gas and electricity, mining, transport and telecommunications) would rank in any big-league table of public and private enterprise, yet be insignificantly multi-national and of little use for regional development since they are geologically or geographically specific to national economies.

What is needed is a combination of both quantitative and qualitative factors, especially for the interregionally mobile manufacturing sector, and also for 'head-office' (or those services as in banking and insurance which can serve a national market from particular regional locations, for example credit-card computer centres). In the E.E.C. case attention would have to be paid to the sizeable multi-national operating on a relatively small scale in the Community rather than elsewhere in the world economy, such as some of the U.S. electronics companies.

The criteria for a new Community location-controls policy for multi-nationals could parallel the British Industrial Development Certificates policy, with the qualification that x per cent of jobs should be specified as a target location for the big-league firms concerned. In a run-in period, such a policy could start with the European top 500 (including foreign multi-nationals), followed by up to the top 1000 European companies. Such a policy would make a considerable advance in making private business more responsible for the social costs of regional under-development in Western Europe.

The location criteria which should be adopted for leading firms can distinguish between various stages of the product cycle. In other words, any policy which is capable of proving effective in controlling the location of leading firms need not impose the same criteria on all the products of that firm, nor on plant at differing stages of the product cycle. There is a considerable case for allowing a more central-area location for that plant representing the early innovation stages of production. In other words, for that stage of the product cycle in which the specific form of the product and production techniques had not been fully ironed out, there is a case for location in individual cases near either a research establishment or a metropolitan social centre (which companies found important for the retention of their middle management). In the mass-production stage where both the product and techniques of production had been ironed out, there would be a case for the location of plant in major centres of unemployment in order to assure sufficient employment provision for the companies. In the mature stages of the product where production itself had become routinised and skill requirements were at their lowest, more dispersed locations could be undertaken by such companies without significant location costs, and with major socio-economic benefits in preventing the decline of dispersed communities.

Harnessing the location of leading firms would ensure that the benefits of soundly based, high-productivity enterprise were registered in less-developed regions. On the other hand, of course, it would not ensure that the disadvantage of intra-sectoral backwash effects on indigenous firms in the L.D.R. was not simply felt more quickly and with more disastrous effects for their longer term growth or survival unless supplementary policies were employed. The basic aim of such policies should be to ensure that positive rather than negative linkages were established between M.D.R. incomers and resident L.D.R. firms where the latter were of sufficient size to be able to provide inputs for incoming firms of the requisite quality and price, that is to ensure that such local firms could be 'led' rather than 'backwashed' by the incoming leaders. To take Averitt's terminology, the incoming 'centre' firms (or in practice the plant located in the L.D.R. by such firms) should be linked with the 'peripheral' L.D.R. firms.[1] Or, in Perrouxist terminology, the growth promotion effects of large-scale, fast-expanding *firmes motrices* should be linked with satellite supplier firms which draw their market strength as well as market orientation from the new breed of incomers.[2]

Meso–Micro Linkage

Several virtuous effects would follow from a policy which concentrated on inter-firm linkages between incoming meso-economic firms and micro-economic L.D.R. firms provided that it was not simultaneously attempted to combine this policy with an inflexible policy of an inter-industry or industrial complex input–output type. One of the most important limitations of input–output analysis is the failure to 'fill' the industry boxes of the matrix with particular firms. A basically static linkage is sketched, and then shelved for academic enlightenment. The reason in many cases is not simply the difficulty of dynamising a technique which depends on fixed coefficient assumptions in a world of changing techniques, but the assumption that indirect incentives to existing regional firms or to national firms to locate in the region will be sufficient to ensure that the location and expansion on desired inter-sectoral proportions actually takes place. In industrial-complex analysis the technique is further handicapped by the assumptions (1) that firms need to locate in the same area in order to gain from 'technological' external economies, and (2) that they will do so simultaneously on the precise coefficients specified by the industrial complex model. Assumption (1) is misplaced since the principal external economies hitherto assumed to be technological in character amount in practice to pecuniary external economies of location, and under modern transport and communications conditions these can be served in most cases as easily in a dispersed as a concentrated location. Assumption (2) would demand not only precise control over location, but also the simultaneous location of firms on precisely the scale specified by the input–output coefficients.

By contrast, a policy which aimed at securing local inputs where possible for incoming leader firms could be wider ranging both in the alternative locations which it offered, and in the number of local firms which could be specifically linked to the new incoming investment. It could be feasibility orientated in the sense that it would deal with particular firms, management, plant and equipment, known past production achievement, and identifiable expansion potential. Administrative personnel in regional development departments and agencies could be employed to fulfil the practical business of ensuring that the respective management and local representatives met, specified their needs over given time periods, drew up contracts and acted upon them. The information available from intersectoral and interregional input–output models might be taken into account in providing the broader structure desired for the region in relation to the national economy over a given period of time, but the essential elements of the policy would remain 'actual' rather than 'hypothetical' firms. Once agreements had been reached and inter-firm linkages established, this information could be fed into a dynamised input–output model and provide an indication of the likely shortfall, sector for sector, for the desired structure at a given terminal period. Depending on size and manageability, the regionalised matrix could distinguish between (1) incoming plant and their established L.D.R. firm linkages, and (2) resident L.D.R. firms with sufficient potential for linkages with incoming plant from M.D.R. firms, for which priority linkages should be established.

One of the virtues of employing input–output analysis on the basis of actual coefficients between firms in this manner would be the extent to which they included potential changes in production coefficients, and enabled a tracing of inter-sectoral effects to be secured for the two cases in which they were most important – between M.D.R. incomers and L.D.R. firms. The technique could still tend to become an end in itself if policy-makers lacked the political will and social support for regional planning as a continuous on-going dimension of new national planning. For one thing, it would be crucial to secure advance information from leading firms in the meso-economic sector on their location forecasts as part of a wider forecasting information basis including investment, jobs, prices and trade. Without such background information, the use of new regional input–output at the meso-economic level could exert only a partial and local effect rather than span the present gap between the micro and macro levels.

Clearly the size of firms in the L.D.R. would be important in the extent to which they could provide linkages with incoming plant. A predominance of small-scale laggard firms in an under-developed area or region would mean that much of the complementary linkages would have to be established in the first instance between different plant of incoming firms. But this would not mean to say that a structural reorganisation and expansion programme for laggard firms could not be pursued in the L.D.R. in order to build up the fabric of small- and medium-sized firms in the region. In Italy this has been done by a special State Holding Company for small-and medium-sized enterprise in the South – E.F.I.M. In Britain the Industrial Development Executive, established in 1972, was supposed to fulfil such a role for any viable firm in a Development Area.[3] But, in practice, since leader firms did not need the money or advice which the I.D.E. could offer, this led the I.D.E. being preoccupied with 'led' or 'laggard' firms. The I.D.E. certainly lacked sufficient leverage on national leader firms to ensure meso–micro linkage in the sense described above. This is partly explained by the hold which leading British companies have on the regional policy-makers (especially the blackmail threat to locate abroad, and the degree of internal division of labour and production in multi-nationals). Means of countering this are spelled out in the next chapter.

Balanced Regional Structure

Comparative international data indicates a long-term decline in agricultural employment in the mature capitalist economies, an incipient slowing down of the rate of manufacturing employment, and an expansion of employment in services. The market mechanism cannot be relied upon to assure a smooth adjustment to regional full employment, either between or within these three main sectors. The main reasons relate to the location characteristics of the sectors themselves, and to the location behaviour of leading firms in regionally mobile or 'footloose' sectors.

Only manufacturing and certain 'head-office' services constitute regionally mobile sectors. Mining, agriculture, and forestry are self-evidently location-tied. Similarly, basic industry, or what are sometimes called the service industries, are location-tied: i.e. power generation and distribution (gas, oil and electricity), and telecommunications (telephones and post-office services). There is no point in trying to double the rate of employment increase in a major region by doubling the rate of expansion of any of these sectors alone. The result will simply be under-utilised social overhead capital. In the service sector proper, only the head offices of companies serving the national or international market have any real mobility potential. Other services such as local transport, wholesale and retail outlets, personal services, bank and insurance branches and so on, are, by definition, location-tied. Manufacturing is the key sector in terms of capacity to shift new jobs and generate supplementary jobs in local services through the employment multiplier. Brown distinguished manufacturing as 'basic' industry and the rest as 'non-basic' in the results of his N.I.E.S.R. study, and concluded that movement of manufacturing jobs into a region will eventually create 80 per cent more jobs in local non-basic employment. The process is slow if left to the free working of the market mechanism. It may take up to ten years. But, in addition, the converse is not true to any great extent: the creation of new non-basic employment in local services will not by itself induce or pull 100 manufacturing jobs into a region.[4]

For such reasons any policy seeking to ensure long-term employment viability in a problem region should be based essentially on bringing in new manufacturing, supplemented in some cases by head-office employment in services. The fall-off in the rate of growth of manufacturing employment in the mature capitalist economies means that this is going to be more difficult in the future, and strengthens the case for stronger powers of control over the location of leading companies. Also, multi-national spread of capital and jobs in the last fifteen years has led to an acceleration of 'runaway' industries in precisely those relatively labour-intensive manufacturing sectors which are most necessary for regional development: light electrical engineering and electronics, plastics, modern synthetic textiles and natural fibre textile production, and so on. This problem is compounded by the fact that many companies are increasingly shifting head-office or general office services in banking, finance and insurance to tax havens rather than to problem regions where employment is declining in traditional sectors such as coalmining or shipbuilding. These havens are frequently high income areas (for example Switzerland, Lichtenstein and Jersey) and have little need of the income and employment generated by the incoming financial companies. In other tax-haven cases, such as the Bahamas, the financial offices of multi-national companies and banks constitute enclaves in a primitive economic structure, with classic 'dualistic' results. The twin factors of (1) fall-off in the rate of manufacturing employment growth, and (2) multi-national rather than multi-regional location of the jobs best suited for regional develop-ment, herald a coming employment crisis for problem regions in the mature capitalist economies unless new policy instruments can be evolved to ensure at least selective controls over the location of leading manufacturing firms.

Significant differences in the rate of growth of both product and employment are found between 'traditional' and 'modern' manufacturing. The former includes food, drink and tobacco, clothing and leatherwork, furniture and woodwork, and non-metallic mineral products. The latter includes textiles (where these were synthetic fibre and compound based), metallurgy, engineering, chemicals, chemical products, rubber and paper. Within 'modern' manufacturing the two spearhead sectors with the fastest employment and product growth were engineering and chemicals and chemical products. These in turn include the broad range of heavy and light mechanical engineering, electrical engineering, electronics, para-chemicals, plastics and pharmaceuticals. It is seen from Cacace's breakdown of capital cost per employee that steel, primary chemicals and their derivatives, cement and rubber all involve a higher cost 'per capita' than the average for manufacturing as a whole, while the 'traditional' manufacturing industries involve the lowest capital cost. But the two spearhead manufacturing sectors of engineer-ing and chemical products (with the exception of steel, primary chemicals and immediate derivatives) all entail a lower average capital cost per employee than manufacturing as a whole.[5]

The question of over-all sectoral balance only becomes important with relatively large regions. There is no clear-cut boundary in geographical space which fits the autonomous regions in much of the inter-industry analysis of an in-put–output type. Besides, the availability of data on which to estimate interregional and inter-industry input-output depends on the region itself being either a nation state, or sharing the essential data-gathering characteristics of a nation state (e.g. an island region such as Sicily in which some trade figures with the mainland were available). The principle of sectoral balance becomes more important the closer the region itself corresponds to at least one of the features of the 'optimum currency' region: limited net emigration, *or* emigration insufficient to reduce regional population levels. This gives a sufficiently wide range. Such a region lies somewhere between Monaco and the world capitalist economy. The optimum currency area formula gives no golden key to this problem. But it does show that no region could benefit from an independent currency unless it contained a sufficiently balanced domestic economy to be able to offset losses from higher import prices with gains from lower export prices following devaluation. The principle of sectoral balance for such large regions obtains whether or not it is politically possible to give them an independent currency. And these factors obtain independently of the wider problem of ensuring that meso-economic companies in the multi-national sector actually do respond to exchange-rate changes once undertaken or induced by floating.

It certainly can be questioned whether Scotland is big enough to fulfil such minimum size requirements. The South of Italy, by contrast, with a population nearly equivalent to Benelux, clearly could do so, like those E.E.C. economies which still have independent currencies, but would become nation-regions in a single-currency area if monetary union is introduced in the Community. No such region can afford to neglect the manufacturing base for induced local services employment if it wishes to attempt employment and income levels comparable with central factor-inflow regions (either North Italy in the Italian case, or the Rhine axis in the E.E.C. case). If the initial sectoral structure of the region shows a clear under-representation of manufacturing, this is likely to be most marked in 'modern' manufacturing, and within it in the spearhead sectors of engineering and chemical products. In order to ensure a re-balancing of regional productive structure, it would therefore be necessary to unbalance the existing structure in favour of modern manufacturing in general, and the spearhead sectors in particular. This would provide the base for faster-than-average job and income generation not only in industry but also in promotion of local services.

For a major region these should be the main guidelines for

sectoral strategy. They would be qualified by the meso-economic and multi-national dimension in sectoral structure, where the effectiveness of any strategy could depend in practice on a handful of giant companies spanning several industries and services. They would change over time with the rise of new manufacturing industries; the relative success of national industries in international trade; the potential for long-term growth of income and employment in specialised services such as tourism; the suitability of particular urban areas as centres for head-office dispersal in services rather than manufacturing employment, and so on. In other words, they would guide the strategic decision-making for the structure of the region, rather than constrain it by adhering to rigid rules. For major nation states such guidelines would apply to relatively large regions and initially be constrained by the feasibility of data collection and processing. But in this case, as in others, the new regional planning would gain from information collection from leading meso-economic firms and from new instruments for precise location of such leaders within the region. This would make possible advance information for a rolling regional matrix rather than the *ex post* rigidity of regional input–output models. Target proportions for the location of the main categories of manufacturing and mobile services could be established for a given planning period, advancing on the model of the Italian targets for state enterprise in the South.

Beyond the Growth Centre

This leaves open the question of the desirable location pattern of manufacturing enterprise *within* main regions, and the criteria to be employed in locational policy. False hopes have been generated in this area by industrial-complex analysis based on input–output, which has reinforced the main weaknesses of the Perroux growth-pole concept. For one thing, spatial-complex analysis imposes enormous demands on policy-makers and administrators, requiring controlling the precise size of plant, the scale of output, and the sale of that output to local buyers in the complex. But in any case the assumption that proximity is necessary for such plant to secure scale economies is misplaced, and the tailoring of plant to fit the input–output coefficients of such a model is unnecessary. If one can break the spell of this type of analysis and return to the basic objectives of regional development policy, the question of criteria can be simplified considerably. These objectives can be identified as the reduction of unemployment and income differentials between the main national regions. The precise indirect effects of employment in one or more plants is difficult to estimate with precision. But, in the first instance, the provision of that employment itself is not. Further, if priority is made for investment in sectors with higher-than-average rates of growth of product and employment, such as metal-processing and chemicals, the intermediate and final income creation should contribute to the reduction of disparities between the main regions rather than either simply enabling the region to hold its own, or allowing it to fall behind the faster-growing region.

To operate on the reduction of unemployment in the problem region, a spatial economic map could be drawn up which would identify the relative degree of unemployment and the absolute number of unemployed in different areas, and provide a basis for the determination of where plant should be located. Since the Luttrell and the I.R.I. Società Autostrade evidence have indicated that fast-growth industries can be successfully dispersed, the main criterion for the scale of location in any particular area would be the unemployment reduced through one or more plant rather than their scale in relation to each other.[6] That is, firms could be allowed to locate plant on a scale of their own choice, but in a location determined by the government department responsible for locational controls. In order for this to be effective, firms should be obliged to submit their expansion programmes, for a given medium-term period, to the department concerned, which could then estimate the total and particular employment creation available to the region over that period, and determine precisely which plant should be located in which areas. The policy could be sophisticated by demographic projection and by improvement of unemployment estimation, taking under-employment into account, but existing unemployment statistics would give a sufficiently workable framework in the first instance for the policy to be applied.

It will be evident that the criterion of unemployment reduction, in the first instance, considerably simplifies the question of whether to concentrate location in a few large centres or to disperse it more widely. If a firm needs 15,000 workers for a new plant, such as the Alfa-Romeo project at Pozzuoli near Naples, it will clearly need to locate in an urban area in which 15,000 employees are available. This availability would also depend on the existence of more than 15,000 unemployed, granted that employers should expect to be able to select to some extent on the basis of expecting a given number of years service after training, as well as physical fitness and adaptability. Therefore the availability of such a labour force would require an urban centre of considerable size. In addition, the same percentage of unemployed per thousand of population clearly would entail more unemployed in larger centres. On this twin basis of sufficient minimum labour for very large plant, and the reduction of the absolute level of unemployed, the larger urban centres would be likely to be priority areas for controlled location. Other factors would also tend to identify larger urban centres as priority areas in the early stages of a development programme. Whatever plans there may be for the ultimate provision of modern transport and power networks, water supply and communications throughout most of the region, there will be resource and time constraints on the rate at which it can be provided. Meanwhile, adaptation and improvement of infrastructure of this type in larger urban centres which are already better endowed is likely to yield quicker results.

However, there are various costs from promoting the growth of larger urban centres at the expense of more isolated locations. One of the clearest is the cost of social overhead capital provision per additional worker in larger communities. For a community with more than 200,000 inhabitants, the cost on SVIMEZ estimates of public services was nearly three times that in communities of only 30,000, and four times as much in the case of public utilities alone.[7] By social cost criteria, though this clearly would not be the only relevant factor, it would clearly be desirable to restrain further expansion. Investment in social overhead capital clearly would be necessary and desirable as a priority in employment creation. But, in terms of long-run resource utilisation, it would be advisable to aim at the provision of sufficient infrastructure to permit the reduction of existing unemployment, and that projected as likely

in the medium term, rather than continue with its indefinite
and increasingly costly provision.[8]

One of the principal reasons for aiming to direct industrial
employment to centres of less than 200,000 population would be
lower social overhead capital costs. But, in addition, there would
be a long-run benefit to the economy as a whole from providing
industrial employment opportunities in such dispersed locations
in depressed or under-developed regions. This would have a
beneficial inter-sectoral as well as inter-area migration effect, by
not only reducing labour inflow into the larger centres with
identifiable congestion costs, but also reducing the expansion of
employment in services in those centres where labour inflow has
exceeded industrial employment opportunities and does not
contribute to either directly productive activity or productivity
in the region or the economy as a whole. Moreover, on the basis
of Ackley's evidence that labour is more willing to migrate from
agriculture to industrial employment the nearer the provision of
that employment to the area of outflow, there would also be a
long-run benefit from accelerating the decline of working
population in agriculture.[9] In E.E.C. economies where the
Common Agricultural Policy maintains high agricultural support prices in order to provide a relatively high standard of
living to the working population in agriculture, this could in due
course result in substantial savings.

If these arguments indicate that government locational policy
should be directed to the provision of industrial employment in
relatively dispersed locations, the question of determining the
desirable degree of such dispersion remains. It has already been
suggested that the absolute level of unemployment should be
taken as the principal index of where to locate and how much
employment to provide. The very small size of plant which the
I.R.I. Società Autostrade evidence shows can be successfully
located in relatively isolated Italian communes, *if* these are near
a motorway with usable access roads, indicates that a policy
of dispersion could include hitherto neglected pockets of
unemployment. Olivier Guichard has suggested such a policy of
'micro-aménagement' for France: 'Planning should sometimes
take on problems which, specifically, concern an urban quarter,
a rural commune, a town of 10,000 inhabitants, or a multi-
communal agglomeration.'[10] Further, in estimating the extent to

which social infrastructure or a modern transport system should be extended, the degree of certainty in employment creation permitted by specific locational controls is of considerable advantage. At present most transport cost–benefit analysis has only been able to include reduced transport costs, increased traffic flows, increased receipts from higher rateable value and reduced congestion in the benefit account. But if the state is incurring unemployment-benefit costs from unemployed but employable labour in relatively isolated locations, the net saving from the guaranteed creation of a given number of new jobs could be estimated and offset against the cost of further investment.

CHAPTER 8

BEYOND STATE CAPITALISM?

Public versus Private Enterprise

The main emphasis of the new policy imperatives so far outlined lies in control of the location of firms. A government need not control the location of all firms, nor need impose the same general rule for location on all stages of a firm's production cycle. But the key to unlocking the underlying imbalance between the regional distribution of capital and labour lies in the control of capital. Labour will not move from problem areas in sufficient quantity to offset even major differences in unemployment and income, while capital not only tends to stay, either at its original location or near metropolitan areas, but also increasingly locates abroad in tax or labour havens in the Third World. In other words, quite apart from the political infeasibility of major involuntary population migration, this would have to be into centre areas which already tend to be over-developed in terms of social congestion costs. And even this emigration would not absorb the labour reserve of problem regions so long as leading national firms could up and away to the much lower-cost labour havens of the Third World. At the same time, any regional policy which is seriously attempting to cope with differences in the structural composition of main regions will have to control the location of leading firms in the meso-economic sector. It is the competitive inequality between such firms and other national and regional companies which underlies the differences in regional growth rates for the same industries.

The problem posed by multi-national versus multi-regional firms is intensifying with the rise of meso-economic power and the trend to monopoly in the mature capitalist economies. It erodes the pull effect of Keynesian policies such as the regional devaluation intended to follow from the Regional Employment

Premium in Britain, or regional incentives through capital grants and aids. General controls over location such as the British Industrial Development Certificate are least effective for the meso-economic firms they most need to catch. They are also most cumbersome for the smaller micro-economic firms they need least – both in terms of administrative costs and the adjustment costs imposed on small firms which cannot easily cope with a more distant location.

The Italians have found an instrument for harnessing meso-economic power to regional development through control over the location of public meso-economic enterprise. This is the state enterprise of the I.R.I.- and E.N.I.-type. The contribution of these state companies to the development of the Mezzogiorno emerges most clearly from a breakdown of the value added and employment in the South over nearly twenty years since 1950, which shows that it is only in those sectors where state enterprise is significantly represented that the region has been able to improve its share of national output and employment.[1] This resulted mainly from the location controls imposed on state enterprise by legislation in 1957 which required them to put 40 per cent of their total investment and 60 per cent of their investment in new plant in the region. Since 1968 the controls have been raised to 60 per cent of investment and all new plant, with the required area extended to include certain areas in the depressed Centre-North of the country.[2]

State Capitalist Planning

In this way the Italians have rediscovered the regional development instrument so strongly favoured in the early economic history of the United States – State Capitalism. The positive results achieved through state-enterprise location in the South has impressed a variety of other countries faced with decreasingly effective regional policies, and has promoted the introduction of State Holding Companies in France and Belgium, the reorganisation of the main Swedish public enterprises into the new Statsföretag, and West German proposals for a new State Holding company based on an enlarged VIAG (United Industrial Companies).[3]

State Capitalism is a mixed blessing for liberal capitalists.

Liberal capitalism in the sense of freedom for private enterprise to choose its own location has proved the crucial base of the modern regional problem. Negative intervention on liberal capitalist lines, such as locational controls, are increasingly eroded by the trend to multi-national location by big-league meso-economic firms in mobile manufacturing industry. In principle, this can be offset by the state itself becoming a capitalist and ensuring that its own enterprise in mobile manufacturing locates in problem regions and areas. But, in practice, State Capitalism has tended to play a supplementary role to private capitalism. It has concentrated in the basic industries and services of the Western European economies, where the large scale of projects or a co-ordinated monopoly solution has been necessary to ensure the provision of social services and inputs for manufacturing industry. Until recently, the scale of production necessary to enter and survive in manufacturing was quite small, and the sector was left mainly to private enterprise. Leverage from private enterprise on the state, plus the need to cope with increasing inflation, has resulted in the use of public enterprise in basic industry and services as a low-cost provider of goods and services to client private enterprise. The result has been (1) a marked concentration of public enterprise in heavy industry and services, with high capital intensity and low regional development potential, and (2) low profits or losses in public enterprises which have not been free to price on a cost-plus or similar profit-making basis.

This situation suited private enterprise very well. It meant that their own production costs were subsidised by the public sector while at the same time public enterprise appeared incompetent or inefficient to the uninformed through its inability to make profits because of price controls. But with the rise of meso-economic capital and the increasing flight of runaway industries to foreign labour and tax havens, the underlying nature of the regional problem has been increasingly aggravated during a period in which modern capitalist states have been under pressure to alleviate the social and political costs of regional imbalance and national unemployment. The early success of Keynesian policies in the immediate post-war period, before multi-nationalisation and the meso-economic trend eroded their base, encouraged unions and opposition parties (mainly socialist) to press for further modifications of the liberal capitalist system. The example of the Italian state enterprises in the South of Italy showed the unions that regional unemployment and redundancy could be offset by bringing viable manufacturing enterprise into the South with negligible or no location costs. The union and party pressures on the state enterprises came to include the reasonable demands that the main holding companies diversify from basic industry and services into less capital-intensive and higher-growth-generating modern manufacturing.[4]

At the same time, political and union protest in Italy brought monopolistic private companies such as FIAT, Pirelli and Olivetti under increasing pressure to locate a higher proportion of their investment in the main problem region of the South. The government harnessed this in 1968 through new Planning Agreements, or Programme Contracts, whereby such companies submitted the main elements of their medium-term corporate programmes to the Ministry of the Budget and Economic Programming. The Ministry assessed the regional implications of the programmes and bargained out the location of a proportion of their investment in the South and other depressed areas of the Centre-North In principle, the location requirements from public enterprise introduced in 1957, and intensified in 1968, left state firms free to choose their own location in the same regions and areas. But, in practice, both state enterprise and leading private enterprise became subject to government control over the specific location of major projects. In other words, Italy pioneered the application of specific location controls as the main means of trying to ensure that leading firms were harnessed to the benefit of problem regions. In the same year (1968) both the French and Belgian governments introduced Programme Contracts of a similar kind, combining a formal co-operative framework in which firms were invited to submit their medium-term programmes to the planning authorities, with a *de facto* pressure on them to do so if they wished to secure any trade-off from other aspects of government economic policy. However, in practice the Belgian planners have found that they lack real leverage on leading multi-national companies through such contracts. Philips and Siemens have played along, and pioneered their use in Belgium.

But there is a strong feeling that the main result of the new agreements has been a good public-relations exercise for the companies, window-dressing what they probably would have been prepared to do in the first place with or without the new procedures. (The Belgians in fact have four main variants of the Programme Contracts procedure. Programme Contracts proper, which mainly concern prices; Progress Contracts, concerning research, development and government purchasing; Prototype Contracts, covering advanced technology projects such as nuclear power and uranium, which are state contracts involving a public shareholding, and Management Contracts, which involve state consultancy, state managers for some companies and the injection of public money into companies. The Siemens and Philips examples cited above came under the Progress Contracts procedure.)

In France, officials of the Finance and Economics Ministry for some time have shown their skills at ignoring most E.E.C. regulations on freedom of capital movements. But this has not been of much help in preventing foreign multi-national penetration of selected areas in the French economy, and in particular the Paris region. So far the government clearly has been prepared to tolerate this aggravation of regional imbalance in return for the assumed trade-off in terms of new technology. But if the present unemployment and inflation in France persist for long, this may well affect the investment confidence of leading firms in the private sector. Such a fall-back in the expansion of private capital would intensify the problems posed by multi-nationals for the French government and strengthen the need for new policy instruments to back the Programme Contracts procedure.[5]

In practice, only Italy in Western Europe today has a sufficiently large and widespread distribution of state enterprise to be able to countervail free location by multi-national firms. This has arisen partly through the diversification of the State Holding Companies through the 1960s into entirely new manufacturing industries such as electronics, chemical fertilisers and para-chemical products, food processing, wholesale and retail distribution, nuclear-power engineering, civil-aircraft construction, telecommunications, data processing and so on. It also has followed from the state taking control through I.R.I.

and E.N.I. of the huge Montedison conglomerate, concentrated in chemicals and pharmaceuticals, following the mismanagement of the merger of Edison and Montecatini after the compensation of the former with electricity nationalisation in 1962 and the funds shortage in the Montecatini company. West Germany would have had such a base for coping with the multi-nationals if it had introduced the 1970 Möller proposals for a reorganised VIAG. Britain also could secure such a base if the Labour government in the mid-1970s makes a reality of the National Enterprise Board as conceived by the Labour Party in opposition. But, at present, there is every sign that the British government is lapsing into a classic state capitalist role for the N.E.B., reacting defensively on a salvage basis for big and small companies in difficulties, rather than pioneering new public leadership in the meso-economic sector as a direct means of promoting regional development.[6] To date Italy remains both the main pace-setter in the new regional use of public enterprise as a direct development instrument, and the use of such enterprise as a lever to ensure co-operation from leading private-enterprise firms in regional development.

National and Regional Development

If countries are to follow the Italian lead in the use of state enterprise they must *both* introduce sufficient public ownership of selected leading firms through manufacturing, *and* ensure that a strategic framework is adopted in which policy tactics and techniques of analysis can serve the solution of main dimensions of the regional problem. This would necessitate a change in key features of the present policy for economic and monetary union in the E.E.C. None of it will happen simply by intellectual enlightenment. A more widespread appreciation of the extent to which the modern capitalist firm lies at the heart of the problem, and a demystification of some of the main theories and techniques may play some part in loosening the hold of market mythology on regional policy-makers. But the real pressures for change will come through a heightening of the present contradictions in the process of regional, national and international resource allocation under liberal capitalist policies. In practice, the pursuit of higher stages of monetary integration in the E.E.C. is unlikely to be accompanied by progress in policies for 'positive' integration, mainly because nation states oppose the loss of economic sovereignty involved. At the same time their effective sovereignty in regional policy is being eroded at an increasing rate by the rise of meso-economic power and multi-national versus multi-regional location. The meso-economic trend increases the inequalities in competition between leading and lagging firms, with the latter mainly located in problem regions and areas. The multi-national trend means the shifting abroad of the jobs most suited to cope with regional problems at home.

Liberal capitalist governments are unlikely to introduce the scale or spread of new public enterprise necessary to change the balance of public and private power, and thereby put themselves in a position to cope with the increasing scale of the regional problem. At best they will partly offset it by *ad hoc* measures which will involve the nationalisation of some companies in the public eye which are threatened with multi-national takeover, and increased location of their investment in problem regions. But no such government outside Italy began with the inheritance of a wide-ranging spread of state companies such as the Italians secured with the establishment of I.R.I. in 1933 (when the new State Holding Company took over the shares held by three of the main national banks in an extensive range of manufacturing and service sectors). Also, none of them has had the advantage of the organic growth of an I.R.I. over forty years, or of an E.N.I. over twenty years. They will have to do more, and do it faster, simply to catch up with (1) the regional development capacity of the Italian State Holdings, and (2) the indirect role of such Holdings in giving government real leverage over leading private enterprise in regional policy. In practice, this is likely to be achieved either by socialist or social-democratic governments under organised pressure from their respective labour movements. (The new public ownership proposed in the 1972 common programme of the French Communist and Socialist parties, and the 1973 programme of the British Labour Party offer the clearest potential for such a strategy in Western Europe outside Italy.) It also would be such Left-of-Centre governments which would be likely to oppose the present trend of the European Community in regional policy, and ensure a nation-state base for regional development in an internationalist E.E.C. framework.

It is in such a context that it makes sense to specify the manner in which extended public enterprise could be used to change the present imbalance between public and private power and restore initiative to governments in regional policy-making. The governments concerned must ensure a range of public enterprises through the main manufacturing and service sectors. The rationale for such new public ownership is not likely to be limited to regional development alone. One of its virtues is the extent to which public enterprise in manufacturing and modern services can contribute to other aspects of government economic policy. These include (1) a direct instrument for counter-cyclical policy or the transmission of government expenditure to offset a recession in private-enterprise investment; (2) long-term investment of a kind which private enterprise will not hazard, especially in basic industry or advanced technology enterprise; (3) an instrument for restraining the rate of price increases in the key manufacturing sector, or charges in the modern services sector; (4) import promotion and export substitution, especially in areas where multi-national companies are not fully responding to exchange-rate changes as foreign-trade instruments. These amount to specific dimensions of a general strategy for national planning based on leading firms, and countervailing private multi-national enterprise. Any strategy which has grasped that the regional problem is the spatial dimension of inequalities and imbalance within the economy as a whole, caused by divergences between private and social interests, will ensure that such use of leading public enterprise is spatialised in a planning framework covering international, national and regional policy.

The previous argument on regional structure and the location of plant was based on more selective and more specific control of the location of leading firms. This can be achieved directly through new public enterprise in manufacturing and modern services, and indirectly through the leverage which this would ensure in causing private enterprise to fall into line with government economic strategy. But *both* are necessary if the government is to be put in a position to make a reality of the specific location planning which has been pioneered in Italy through the Programme Contracts system. And this system itself must be elevated to a more central place in national and regional policy, providing the basis of the new *ex ante* techniques of analysis on which planning the future of problem regions depends.

Such a new planning mechanism, based on leading firms in the meso-economic sector, should operate for both public and private enterprises. If gains are to be secured from a more precise control of the location of plant, it must be imperative rather than indicative in character for the meso-economic leaders. This would mean a bargaining process between the planning authorities and leading firms, in which both sides stated the merits of a range of possible cases for the firms and local areas. Regional and local authorities, and the interested unions, should take part in this bargaining process if it is to be democratically based and economically efficient. This is the kind of tripartite bargaining procedure established for national planning in the Labour Government's 1974 Industry White Paper.[7] But the government must have the final say on the specific location of leading public and private companies. And in the case of recalcitrance by leading private firms which threaten to locate abroad if they are not allowed a location of their choice at home, the government must be prepared to return the challenge by giving notice that it may take the firm into public ownership. To some extent the Italians have found that the possibility of such nationalisation is sufficient to ensure the co-operation of leading private firms. But this partly reflects the already established position of the Italian State Holding Companies over a relatively long period of time. In other countries, such as France and Britain, the government may well have to make an example of one or more meso-economic companies not brought into an initial public ownership package, simply *pour encourager les autres.* This new meso-economic strategy for the regions should be matched by complementary macro-and micro-economic policies: these would be (1) interregional; (2) inter-sectoral; (3) intra-sectoral; and (4) intra-regional.

At the interregional level the main guidelines for the balanced regional use of national resources would be a cost–benefit framework. Such a framework can only be filled by selective case studies operating as indicators for macro regional policy. This will depend partly on building up dossiers on congestion and other social costs in over-developed areas, and the costs of under-employment of resources in less-developed areas. Macro-economic estimates can be made from available regional data on the lines indicated by the Moore and Rhodes study.[8] But the ultimate level at which such policy must operate, and the empirical base from which aggregate indices must be assessed, will remain essentially meso-economic. Its main aim would be to transfer the social costs of pressured resource use in leading regions into social benefits through the fuller use of resources in the less developed. This would be mainly through restraint on the location of the large-scale meso-economic firms in M.D.R.s and the focus of their future expansion in L.D.R.s. Its general aim would be to offset the asymmetry in capital and labour which underlies regional imbalance through a more effective control of the interregional distribution of public and private capital.

Over-all sectoral balance is important mainly at the level of relatively large regions. But the employment of a manufacturing base of some kind for the spontaneous generation of local services remains important for large urban centres as well as for regions as a whole. The exceptions to this principle have already been outlined. But, in general, the ratio of up to 80 local service jobs created by the inflow of 100 jobs in manufacturing is a factor which should guide policy-makers in assessing the prospective employment structure of major urban areas. Much wider scope than previously admitted is possible for the local planning of the inter-sectoral employment multiplier. In other words, more local services employment could be provided faster than the five-to-ten years build up which British evidence suggests is the normal time period for such a 'spread' into services from incoming manufacturing jobs. As with the case of intra-sectoral strategy, this is a question where linkage and job creation should be planned rather than left to the free working of the market alone. The different boundaries between and within sectors will depend mainly on existing national accounts categories and the accounting definitions used in regional and local planning. The important change is to ensure that such planning of linkage is not simply left at the level of statements of intention, or descriptions of income, matrix or employment multipliers which are to be achieved by the market alone, but based on planned linkages between meso-economic leaders and local firms in the micro-economic sector.

The Alfa-Sud (Alfa-Romeo) project at Naples provides a model of the recommended new type of planning. A leading national company in state ownership was obliged to locate a major new venture in one of the main problem areas of the country. This followed a period of bargaining in which the firm had maintained that it could not simultaneously diversify from specialist to mass-production vehicles, and locate the new project in the South. It won this case and expanded high-volume production in the first instance in the North. But when it moved its medium-vehicle Alfa-Sud project to Naples, the parent I.R.I. Holding Company ensured that multiplier leakage from the area and region was minimised through intervening to build up local suppliers for Alfa-Sud. It did this by using one of its own investment banks to scrutinise small- and medium-sized engineering concerns in the area to assess their suitability for expansion to provide inputs and components for the new large-scale project. In the category of automobile production or the wider category of mechanical engineering, such planning of linkage is intra-sectoral. But I.R.I. has also ensured inter-sectoral linkage in the area through directly undertaking the construction of the new site and premises for the plant, new housing for the employees, and so on. In the wider inter-sectoral context, it has built up its own supermarket retailing in the Naples area, wherever possible using products from its own plant in the South. This has included the main range of food products through control of three of the main food-processing and packaging companies in the economy, previously taken into public ownership to prevent takeover by U.S. food companies which intended to use foreign fruit and basic foodstuffs, and sell mainly to the rest of the E.E.C. The result of local planning of the multiplier effects from the Alfa-Sud project alone has already been considerable. Direct employment in the vehicle plant itself is expected to build up to 15,000 in the 1970s. Local employment generated through maximisation of local linkage could ultimately mean a total of 35,000 new jobs.[9]

The Alfa-Sud case shows the direct regional potential of

integrated planning based on leading public-enterprise firms. But what *is* true for public-enterprise leaders can also be *made* true for leading private enterprise provided that the state shifts the balance of initiative and power in its favour by ensuring a sufficient complement of public enterprise in the first place. This is shown by the 'follow-the-leader' effect of Alfa-Sud's location at Naples. From the announcement of the new project in the mid-1960s, both FIAT and Pirelli agreed to new ventures in the South (which they had hitherto neglected relative to the North).[10] To prove most effective, the new public enterprise must be focused in those modern manufacturing sectors which have already been identified as most suitable for promotion of product and employment in problem regions, especially engineering and para-chemical products. In services, the state can only operate directly to bring head-office jobs into a problem region (other than government administration) if it has a share of the main financial institutions, and is informed through its own companies of the real costs and benefits from dispersed location. To extend the local and regional maximisation of multiplier linkages, it would need to be represented in banking and insurance, construction, modern wholesaling and retailing. Such a base is essential if leverage is to be exercised rapidly on leading private enterprise in the same sectors to co-operate with regional Planning Agreements similar to the Italian Programme Contracts, especially where these companies are already multi-national in operation.

Towards Socialist Planning

So far the essence of the argument has been simple enough. Liberal capitalist policies are inadequate to cope with the regional problems caused by liberal capitalism itself. Aids and incentives fail to bite on the leading national and multi-national companies which are most needed to provide a base for the development of problem regions and areas. Consequently the provision of infrastructure and aids, whether dispersed or concentrated in growth poles, fails to pull sufficient investment by leading firms in the meso-economic sector away from metropolitan areas or slow their migration abroad. Indicative planning, and sophisticated techniques such as input–output or industrial-complex analysis, simply disguise the nakedness of liberal capitalist policies with econometric trimmings. To change this imbalance between public and private power, the state itself must, at a minimum, ensure through its own entrepreneurship that direct investment in high-income and employment sectors is brought to problem regions. But it must do so on a substantially wide scale in the relevant industry and service sectors if it is to ensure that it can gain leverage on leading private enterprise in these sectors. It is only in this way that it can countervail the multi-national challenge and ensure sufficient control of location to make techniques of analysis serve operational policies. It needs state entrepreneurship to exercise both direct investment and job creation in problem regions, and mobilise an indirect movement of leading private enterprise in a planned framework into these regions. Without this it has little hope of transforming regional laggards into satellites of leading firms, or creating a sufficiently viable regional economy for local entrepreneurship to flourish at the micro-economic level. (Some of the firms transformed by I.R.I. in the Alfa-Sud case from laggards to led were not even in engineering production at all, but in what had previously been repair and maintenance shops.)

In other words, to solve the modern dimensions of the regional problem the liberal capitalist state must – at a minimum – concern itself in more overt State Capitalism. This is an imperative dictated both by the meso-economic trend, which intensifies the inequalities in regional competition, and by the multi-national spread of leading private enterprise as it seeks to dispose of its surplus and penetrate other markets abroad. But State Capitalism is not a neutral technical device. The very success of state capitalist policies in the Italian case has posed new contradictions in the social and political structure of the economy. When organised labour appreciates that it does not have to be put on the dole, because the State Holdings can both salvage and modernise their enterprise, and when labour in high unemployment areas realises that it does not have to remain unemployed because the state can bring new jobs to them in viable enterprise, new expectations are raised and new demands made on the system. This has been shown since 1968, when the leading unions have pressed for both a more purposive use of state enterprise, and for changed relations between management and labour in leading public and private companies.

In not only Italy, but also France and Britain, the parties of the Left are showing an increasing awareness of the potential of State Capitalism as an instrument for further progress in the transformation of a capitalist system. This could be seen as an increase in the demands for opening the frontier to socialist transition At the present stage it is not clear how programmes adopted in opposition would be implemented (or compromised) if Left-Wing governments were elected to power in future. But, in practice, the liberal capitalist governments which dominate the present European Community are pursuing a strategy which promises to heighten the contradictions of European capitalism as a whole: the federalist proposals of economic and monetary union. The E.M.U. proposals amount in part to a conviction that Europe can only speak with authority among the finance ministers of the world if backed by a single currency; that European companies can only answer the U.S. multi-national challenge by generating a new breed of Euro-multi-nationals, and so on. The principal contradiction dogging the proposals is the fact that monetary integration is far easier to introduce than economic union. Finance ministers stopping the clock at midnight and refreshing themselves into the early morning may well emerge with a decision to abolish their independent currencies and proclaim the dawn of the Euro-franc. They are unlikely to hold office during the period in which such an abolition of exchange-rate changes imposes critical strains on the structure of Western European capitalism. The long-term mystification of capitalist regional theory will be brought home to the governments of Western Europe in a form they at present hardly realise: the nation state as a problem region in a single-currency area.

Several consequences are likely to follow from such a national up-grading of the regional problem with E.E.C. monetary union. One is an increase in the resort to state capitalism by Right-of-Centre governments faced with large-scale redundancies in particular areas. But another consequence is likely to be increased support for such a coherent use of public enterprise as advocated by some of the main socialist parties of the E.E.C. If this is to be translated into effective planning policies, either before or after any monetary union itself, the support of organised labour for such planning will be crucial. Similarly, the new use of public enterprise in a planning framework will be essential if unions are to be able to mount any effective countervailance to multi-national companies.

One of the problems facing unions in action against multi-national companies is lack of information and communication. But there are other problems. Workers' self-management of the concerns through direct takeover runs against the prevailing private-property law, and the order-enforcement powers of the modern capitalist state. Consequently, unions tend to fall into a passive protest role, calling synchronised protest strikes (e.g. Dunlop–Pirelli) rather than mounting a strategy for the transfer of power from multi-national management to themselves. And this is apart from the problem of co-ordinating the production of highly sophisticated companies which tend to split production sequences in different plant around the world, rather than integrate production in self-contained national units which would facilitate worker takeover and self-management.

The pressure for worker self-management differs between capitalist countries. But, in principle, there is no reason why socialist governments should not encourage unions to attempt a high degree of self-management of individual companies, provided that strategic corporate decisions can still be taken in the last instance by national governments in consultation with the national unions. In other words, there are policy areas where national governments have to be able to take ultimate decisions if the interests of the unions and self-managed concerns are to be properly defended, and the possibility of a long-term countervailance to multi-national companies made a reality. They include: (1) the over-all rate of price increase in the company; (2) the contribution of the company to export promotion and import substitution; and (3) the regional location of new plant.[11] The failure to ensure ultimate national control in these areas has seriously compromised the Yugoslav workers' control experiment, and resulted in (1) an over-all rate of inflation in the late 1960s and early 1970s which has matched or surpassed E.E.C. levels; (2) a serious and persistent trend to balance-of-payments deficit; and (3) a continuing regional disparity with which the national authorities have been less able to cope than the state capitalist Italian government. (A fourth main area in which state action is necessary to prevent the emergence of workers' capitalism from workers' control is the national use of taxation as an instrument of revenue raising for public expenditure and income equalisation. But for the same reasons as in a liberal capitalist policy, tax concessions alone cannot be relied upon to attract high revenue self-managed firms to locate major initiatives in problem regions and areas.)

In other words, any socialist strategy for the transformation of the regional problem must avoid an over-devolution of decision-making to worker-managed firms if it wishes to prevent the substitution of private capitalism with worker capitalism. The worker-managed firm can internalise the surplus generated by the firm which previously would have been distributed to the private shareholder, and probably syphoned away to more profitable investment in other regions and areas. But this disposal of the financial surplus from firms is only one part of the imbalance between capital and labour flows which underlies the modern regional problem. The other is the location of the physical surplus in the form of direct investment. If workers in modern manufacturing or mobile services are left free to determine this location, there will be a natural tendency to do so near the original location of the plant or service, as they have done in Yugoslavia.

On the other hand, no socialist party in Western Europe is likely to be able to fulfil the major transfer from private to public power involved in a major extension of new public ownership unless it is both pressured and positively supported by the leading trade unions. The Italian State Holding Companies have shown that it is possible to countervail the main features of the multi-national challenge through action by state enterprise. This has taken various forms including (1) state takeover of firms threatened by foreign multi-nationals, (2) joint ventures with foreign multi-nationals to import their technology and know-how without losing effective control of the enterprise concerned, (3) the takeover of multi-national companies' plant and their diversification into the state sector when the multi-national has decided to pull out of the national economy, and (4) competition with multi-nationals on a long-term expansion basis which has decreased their hold on the national market in important modern manufacturing sectors. In *all* these cases the Italian State Holdings have ensured that the new plant and jobs created are located in the problem regions of the economy. Provided that unions pressing for self-management are willing to agree to ultimate central decision-making in the three areas of prices, trade and location, there is no reason why a socialist government which extends public enterprise as the basis of future regional strategy should not devolve other aspects of corporate decision-making to the new worker-managed firms. In intermediate areas of company policy, a socialist strategy aiming to avoid a new workers' capitalism would ensure that joint agreements were established on a bargaining basis which covered the main elements of policy covered in the Planning Agreements or Programme Contracts system. In key areas of policy such as the freedom to hire and fire management, initiative on new products and techniques, and complete control of the organisation of production and productive relations within companies, the workers in self-managed firms could be given unqualified control, and thereby transform the basis of social and power relations.

Europe and the United States

On the multi-national company front, combined state and worker power on the above lines could advance on the Italian model and recover the initiative. In international organisations such as the E.E.C., and in international relations between the main countries in which multi-nationals operate, new problems would have to be faced and solved if the nation state is to retain the power base essential to cope with the national regional problem through publicly owned and worker-managed enterprise. Besides which, the increasing resort to State Capitalism as a response to the national regional problem throws into question the whole basis of present Community policy towards regions. For one thing, member states of the E.E.C. are increasingly using their own power base to implement 'positive' interventionist policies. This is partly a response to the prevailing 'negative' character of Community policy which, at least till enlargement and the advent of a new regional commissioner, stressed the harmonisation and scaling down of national policies. But it thereby throws up the bigger question whether the Community can ever exercise control over state capitalist instruments. Capitalist it may be, but State it is not. National governments to date have resisted relaxing controls over their own public enterprise, and are not likely to do so in the immediate future. Similarly a location-control policy in the Community is impossible for all enterprises. In other words, national governments will not cede sovereign control which they can exercise on those medium-sized companies too small to achieve multi-national status in the first place, or on those leading national companies which they can keep at home by trade-off, bargaining or the possibility of public ownership.

On the other hand, the Community has considerable scope for new action in regional policy if it can act where member states have already lost sovereignty in location: that is in dealing with leading multi-national companies, especially where these are not mainly controlled by interests based in the member state itself. There are a variety of possible policies which could counter the extent to which multi-national companies play off one member state of the Community against others. One is a Commission scheduling of companies which are effectively multi-national in European operation, in agreement with member governments, and the stipulation of location criteria which such companies should fulfil. This would be a form of European Industrial Development Certificate policy, but acting on multi-nationals rather than all companies. The procedure for scrutiny and vetting of such companies' location might operate through the Commission on lines similar to those which national governments operate through Programme Contracts or Planning Agreements. The other area in which there is scope for new Community action is in multi-national public-enterprise joint ventures, mainly located in Community problem regions. But if progress is to be made in this area it will be slow, and will only be likely given Commission pressure on private multi-nationals to enter into joint ventures with national public enterprise, on the lines pioneered by I.R.I. in the South of Italy.

However, neither a Euro-I.D.C. for multi-nationals, nor a Euro-I.R.I. will get off the ground unless they reinforce the power of the nation state to cope with national regional problems. They must extend sovereignty rather than reduce it if they are to prove effective. In the case of locational planning through a Community Programme Contracts or Planning Agreements procedure, the Commission would have to ensure that its own Contract or Agreement supplemented rather than substituted that of the nation state. The lines for its operation therefore would have to be primarily inter-governmental (on the lines of the Medium-Term Economic Policy Committee) rather than supra-national. Otherwise such a policy would be stalemated for a generation like the European Company Law. Besides which, there must be some sanction for miscreant multi-nationals which parallels the sanction open at a national level to those countries such as Italy which already control a wide-ranging state-enterprise sector. In principle, one possible sanction is clear enough. Multi-nationals which refuse to respect the rules of the Euro-I.D.C. could be taken into public ownership in the various Community countries where they operated, thereby providing a real base for multi-national public enterprise. But, in practice, the only countries which would be likely to take such a step would be under socialist governments clearly committed to new public enterprise as the basis of both national and regional planning, or governments clearly black-mailed by foreign multi-nationals which announced the closure of operations in selected European countries and future expansion in the Third World (on the lines of the infamous Henry Ford announcement on Ford in Britain).

Such a scenario is not likely except in Britain, France or Italy, and it is only likely in these countries if organised labour exercises sufficient pressure on governments to ensure that it is established. On the other hand, such a socialist response to multi-nationals, and the possibility of multi-national public-enterprise joint ventures, will still have to be based essentially on the nation state in an internationalist Community. The process of international integration is unequal in costs and benefits. As already argued, this is no accident. The higher the stage of integration, the closer the nation state moves to the status of a region. Some states, like some regions, will benefit through capital and labour inflow. Others will suffer accelerated loss of factors of production, but are likely to be only minor donors of labour to the inflow areas, which will draw on the labour reserves of more peripheral and less-developed countries

(Portugal, Spain, Greece and Turkey rather than Italy or Scotland). For these reasons the countries on the Rhine axis such as Germany and the Netherlands are likely to continue to gain from higher stages of liberal capitalist integration, and thus to maintain liberal capitalist governments. It is not they, but regional losers from integration such as Italy and Britain, which are likely to press for a move in the Community beyond liberal capitalism, and to take unilateral or multilateral action to set up new public enterprise through the takeover of private multi-nationals.

Such an outcome was already presaged by the recommendation by ex-Chancellor Brandt in November 1972 that the Community should agree to divide into fast and slow streams, with Britain, Italy and Eire falling away from the leader countries in the process of attempting economic union. But it is even more likely if the Community Right-of-Centre governments proceed with monetary union. The advocates of 'positive' integration maintain that monetary union, which is 'negative' in character, should not be introduced without the previous introduction of common industrial and regional policies. But industrial policies which remain at the level of blueprints for promoting European transnational mergers will only create a new generation of Euro-multi-nationals which cannot be harnessed to the needs of Community problem regions unless locational controls are introduced. And this anyway leaves open the whole question of control over the location of non-European multi-nationals – essentially U.S. companies. In other words, any 'positive' integration policy worthy of the name will have to confront both U.S. companies, and behind them the U.S. government.

At first sight it might appear that there is no chance of the U.S. government agreeing to co-operate on such a policy. For instance, if the formula for a Euro-I.D.C. were pursued in practice at the Community level, it would mean obliging multi-national companies to locate x per cent of their world employment in Community problem regions in return for selling y per cent of their world production in the Community. An intermediate policy sanction which the Commission itself could exercise, whether or not multi-nationals then invited a major confrontation at the Community or national level, would be the indication that market access in the Community would be curtailed for those companies which did not play according to the new rules. This would run counter to most of the spirit and much of the letter of GATT rulings. The fact that GATT rulings are outdated in an era of unequal international competition between companies might justify such a policy, but would not be stomached easily by some of the diplomatic and trade officials in Washington.

On the other hand, the glamour departments of federal government have a seamier backside. Internally the United States is increasingly rent by the horrendous regional–urban problem which has penetrated even the ivory tower of Isard's metaphysics. Even without the duplication of economic and racial problems in U.S. cities, the scale of the urban problem would have demanded increased federal intervention. Yet the intervention which is now undertaken is purely cosmetic. It seeks to cope with the problem of adjustment in cities which have suffered major immigration without properly tackling the underlying cause in the regions of labour outflow. Regional specialists such as Hansen have done good work in importing the main elements of the Perroux imbalance analysis to countervail the prevailing policy orthodoxies. But the designation of growth centres or poles in outflow areas will not pull the big companies which dominate the U.S. economy into Appalachia or the Deep South on a scale sufficient to transform the internal U.S. imbalance in job provision. U.S. analysis in this area is still concerned with the optimum size of growth centres and the designation of a critical minimum size after which it is assumed that spontaneous growth will occur.[12] It has mainly been enterprising political scientists and urban specialists who have recommended a cut-off in the size of metropolitan areas through controls. But, as with the case advocated by supporters of the growth-pole concept in the United States, this has not been matched by an appreciation that optimum size needs operational policies if it is to be translated into reality.[13]

The potential for using public enterprise as the basis for a new regional and urban policy in the United States seems very limited. Existing public enterprise in the United States is still very much concentrated in basic services and infrastructure, with varying degrees of direct government control.[14] As

Callender pointed out at the turn of the century, the original and extensive use of state enterprise in laying the foundations for U.S. economic growth have been buried under the mythology of private service of social needs through the free working of the market.[15] Otherwise, the American New Left adopts a neutral or negative posture to public enterprise as an instrument of public policy. Passing allowance is made that it may be of use to socialists in Europe, but in general it is held that it has little radical potential in the United States. The achievement of public enterprise in Italy is arousing a certain amount of new interest, but is still widely dismissed as a freak by-product of fascism. Besides which, U.S. unions are different in character and political strategy from European unions, especially in France and Italy. They represent a relatively smaller proportion of the working population, and this is mainly white, lower middle class, and strongly self-interested in political strategy. The hard hats have not been noted for their restraint of police batons in southern civil-rights marches. This is no accident. It has been a historical role of trade unions to defend their members' interests. For mainly white unions in the United States, this has been a defence partly against the unorganised poor white and black sections of the community for whom they do not want to pay welfare through higher taxes, and partly against job competition and imports from other capitalist economies.

If the U.S. government does in due course extend public enterprise into manufacturing and mobile services as the basis of federal regional policy it will represent a considerable triumph for mind over matter. If it is pioneered it might well be through a joint-venture formula with leading private companies on particular projects, rather than the taboo formula of nationalisation.[16] On the other hand, for various reasons, there is more chance of the federal government coming round to acceptance of a form of locational control over leading U.S. multi-nationals. One reason will be the continuing aggravation of the problems of inner city areas so long as indirect regional policies of aids, infrastructure and designation of growth centres are relied upon. But others concern the additional problems posed for the U.S. government by too much freedom for multi-nationals to locate investment abroad. This strains the national balance of payments and thereby destabilises dollar diplomacy. There would be considerable gains extending beyond domestic and regional policy for a federal government prepared to introduce some form of control over private multi-nationals' location.

Such a policy would mean considerable intervention in the free working of the market mechanism. But, in general, there is no question that the federal government can exercise considerable power on private enterprise under peacetime conditions when pressured by the failure of other policies. For instance, the combination of stagnant investment, high unemployment and inflation gave the lie to various Keynesian orthodoxies in the early 1970s. The federal government snubbed the Keynesians and introduced direct price controls, consciously or unconsciously following the French planning model embodied in the Programme Contracts procedure. Selective controls of the location of leading companies would mean a major challenge to corporate freedom, but would only twist a knife already planted by the counter-inflationary measures. If operated for the top 200 companies which already control some 60 per cent of industrial capital, they would open a real possibility for a transformation of the at present intractable urban and regional crisis in the United States. A joint policy on location with the E.E.C., focused on such leading companies, would prevent multi-nationals from playing off either of these key sales areas against the other. This is a case which European governments faced with major regional problems could urge directly on the United States in their mutual interests.

NOTES AND REFERENCES

Chapter 1

[1] See the evidence of Lord Stokes of British Leyland Motor Holdings (an employer of some 200,000 people) to the Trade and Industry Sub-Committee of the Commons Select Committee on Expenditure, in *Public Money in the Private Sector*, Sixth Report from the Expenditure Committee (H.M.S.O., July 1972).

[2] A.R. Kuklinski, *Criteria for the Location of Industrial Plant*, United Nations; Economic Commission for Europe (Geneva, 1967).

[3] Such a view is most notably sponsored by Ian Little, *A Critique of Welfare Economics* (Oxford University Press, 1956).

[4] Cf. Peter Hall, *The Theory and Practice of Regional Planning* (London: Routledge & Kegan Paul, 1970) pp.13–14.

[5] Bertil Ohlin, *Interregional and International Trade*, first published in English (Harvard University Press, 1933). Further references in this text are to the revised edition, 1967.

[6] Lucien Brocard, *Principes d'économie nationale et internationale*, 3 vols (Paris: Sirey, 1929–31) vol.1, p.11.

[7] Gunnar Myrdal, *Economic Theory and Underdeveloped Regions* (London: Duckworth, 1957).

[8] Gunnar Myrdal, *Asian Drama*, 3 vols (Harmondsworth: Penguin 1970).

[9] Cf. Gunnar Myrdal, *An International Economy* (London: Routledge & Kegan Paul, 1956).

[10] François Perroux, 'Les Espaces Economiques, *Economie Appliquée*, no.1 (1950) translated as 'Economic Spaces: Theory and Applications', *Quarterly Journal of Economics* (1950).

[11] Cf. J.-R. Boudeville, *Les éspaces économiques* (Presses Universitaires de France, 1964) and *Problems of Regional Planning* (Edinburgh University Press, 1966).

[12] Ibid. and La Documentation Française, *Une image de la France en l'an 2000* (1971).

[13] The lack of a common international criterion for urbanisation means that these proportions are not strictly comparable but should be viewed as indications. For instance, the U.S. proportion refers to that population in S.M.S.A.s (Standard Metropolitan Statistical Areas), which must include a city of at least 50,000 persons in a central county, and 75 per cent of labour in non agricultural employment in

contiguous counties. The definition not only is generous on agricultural employment, but also gives rise to anomalies in the case of completely dispersed but non-agricultural high-income areas.

[14] Cf. Edgar Hoover and Joseph Fisher, 'Research in Regional Economic Growth', in *Problems in the Study of Economic Growth*, Universities National Bureau Committee on Economic Research (1949).

[15] Myrdal, *Economic Theory and Underdeveloped Regions*.

[16] A notable exception to this concentration on intra-urban factors is found in John Kain and Joseph Persky, 'The North's Stake in Southern Rural Poverty', in *Rural Poverty in the United States*, Report of the President's National Advisory Commission on Rural Poverty (May 1968).

[17] A framework on which it might be attempted has been sketched in Stuart Holland, *Capital Versus the Regions* (London: Macmillan, 1976) figs 13 and 14.

[18] A.J. Brown, *The Framework of Regional Economics in the United Kingdom* (Cambridge University Press, 1972) pp.83 and 232. This was initially a study undertaken on behalf of the National Institute of Economic and Social Research (N.I.E.S.R.).

[19] See further A.B. Atkinson, *Unequal Shares* (Allen Lane, The Penguin Press, 1972) ch.1.

[20] This is extensively admitted and argued by the N.I.E.S.R. study, despite the fact that it makes little attempt to calculate the role of congestion costs in such imbalanced resource use. See Brown, *Framework of Regional Economics*, especially pp.245ff.

[21] E.E.C. Commission, 'L'évolution régionale dans la Communauté', *Bilan Analytique* (1971).

[22] For the author's own further work in this area cf., *inter alia*, *The Socialist Challenge* (London: Quartet, 1975).

[23] See Stuart Holland (ed.), *The State as Entrepreneur* (London: Weidenfeld & Nicolson, 1972) for an analysis of the role of the I.R.I. State Holding Company in providing a direct regional development instrument in the South of Italy (especially chs 1 and 7). For an earlier study covering both I.R.I. and the other main Italian State Holding Companies see M.V. Posner and S.J. Woolf, *Italian Public Enterprise* (London: Duckworth, 1967).

[24] Cf. Walter Isard, *Location and the Space Economy* (Massachusetts Institute of Technology Press, 1956); *Methods of Regional Analysis* (ed.) (Massachusetts Institute of Technology Press, 1960), and *General Theory: Social, Political, Economic, and Regional*, in association with Tony Smith and others (Massachusetts Institute of Technology Press, 1969).

Chapter 2

[1] This obtains not only through the standard income and inter-industry multiplier effects (matrix multiplier) but also as a result of

what Paul Streeten has called 'consequential investment', for example the expansion of stereo-record sales with the sale of stereo record players. Cf. Paul Streeten, *Economic Integration,* 2nd edn (Leyden: Sijthoff, 1964).

[2] This effect has been analysed for different European nation-regions by Charles Kindleberger in *Europe's Postwar Growth: the Role of Labour Supply* (Oxford University Press, 1967). Kindleberger may have exaggerated the importance of this factor through failure to stress complementary factors in self-sustaining growth in labour-inflow areas, but his analysis is particularly appropriate to both post-war Italy up to the mid-1960s and for West Germany up to the time of the construction of the Berlin Wall.

[3] Cf. Vera Lutz, *Italy: A Study in Economic Development* (Oxford University Press, 1962).

[4] Kuklinski, *Criteria for the Location of Industrial Plant.*

[5] For a critique of the Lutz case in relation to Italy see, *inter alia,* Stuart Holland, 'Regional Under-Development in a Developed Economy', *Regional Studies,* vol.5 (1971).

[6] Karl Marx, *Capital,* vol I (Moscow, Foreign Language Publishing House, 1961) and Holland, *Capital versus the Regions,* ch.2.

[7] John Maynard Keynes, *The General Theory of Employment, Interest and Money* (London: Macmillan, 1936). See also Roy Harrod, *Towards a Dynamic Economics* (London: Macmillan, 1948).

[8] Myrdal, *Economic Theory and Underdeveloped Regions.*

[9] See, *inter alia,* Marina von Neumann Whitman, 'International and Interregional Payments Adjustment', *Princeton Studies in International Finance,* no.19 (1967).

[10] Labour is spatially inelastic in the sense that for any given interregional difference in wages offered, migration will be lower the greater the distance which the migrant must cover to get the better-paid job. For evidence in the Italian case, cf. Gardner Ackley and Luigi Spaventa, 'Emigration and Industrialisation in Southern Italy', *Banco Nazionale del Lavoro Quarterly Review* (June 1962).

[11] Wilson Gee, 'The Drag of Talent out of the South', *Social Forces,* no.15 (1937); John Van Sickle, *Planning for the South* (1943); Umberto Cassinis, 'Il mercato di lavoro', *CENSIS* (1964), and Bruno Pagani, *Mondo Economico,* no.15 (1960).

[12] See further J.F. Gravier, *Décentralisation et Progrès Technique* (1954); and SVIMEZ, *Ricerca sui costi di insediamento* (1967).

[13] Cf., *inter alia,* Advisory Commission on Inter-Governmental Relations, *Urban and Rural America: Policies for Future Growth (1968)* and *U.S. Bureau of the Census, Finances of Municipalities and Township Governments* (1964).

[14] As Bulova's president Harry Henshel has put it, 'we are able to beat foreign competition because we are the foreign competition'. In *Global Reach: the Power of the Multinational Corporations,* Richard Barnet and Ronald Müller (New York: Simon & Schuster, 1974) p.305.

[15] François Perroux, 'La Firme Motrice dans la Région et la Région

Motrice', *Actes du Colloque International de l'Institut de Science Economique de l'Université de Liège* (Brussels, 1961).

[16] John Kenneth Galbraith, *The New Industrial State* (Boston: Houghton Mifflin, 1967).

[17] J.S. Bain, *Barriers to New Competition* (Harvard University Press, 1962) and Paolo Sylos-Labini, *Oligopoly and Technical Progress* (Harvard University Press, 1962), 2nd revised edition 1969.

[18] Robert T. Averitt, *The Dual Economy* (New York: Norton, 1968).

[19] S.J. Prais, 'A New Look at Industrial Concentration', *Oxford Economic Papers* (July 1974).

[20] Monopolies Commission, *A Survey of Mergers* (H.M.S.O., 1970).

[21] Marx, *Capital*, vol. I, p.626.

[22] Derek Channon, *The Strategy and Structure of British Enterprise* (London: Macmillan, 1973).

[23] U.S. Department of Commerce, *Statistical Abstract of the United States* (1973) tables 779 and 780.

[24] Ibid. table 755.

[25] Mary Kaldor has drawn my attention to the fact that the ratio of foreign production to export in the United States in 1971 was $3 \cdot 96$. For Britain in the same year it was $2 \cdot 15$, but for West Germany and Japan $0 \cdot 37$ and $0 \cdot 38$ respectively. Cf. United Nations, *Multinational Corporations in World Development* (1973).

[26] J.S. Bain, *International Differences in Industrial Structure* (Yale University Press, 1966). See also Jörg Huffschmid, *Die Politik des Kapitals, Konzentration und Wirtschaftspolitik in der Bundesrepublik* (Suhrkamp, 1973), ch.2: Michel de Vroey, *Propriété et Pouvoir dans les Grandes Entreprises*, Centre de recherche et d'information socio-politiques (Brussels, 1973); André-Paul Weber, 'L'économie industrielle de 1950 a 1970: Concentration des entreprises et politique économique', *Révue d'Economie Politique* (Sept–Oct 1970).

[27] For impressive evidence on the survival of the individual inventor rather than the small-scale innovator see, *inter alia*, the evidence of Donald Schon in U.S. Senate Sub-Committee on Anti-trust and Monopoly, *Concentration, Invention and Innovation* (May–June 1965) part 3 pp.1206ff.

[28] Bain, *Barriers to New Competition*.

[29] Sylos-Labini, *Oligopoly and Technical Progress*.

[30] The structural factor is stressed in Gavin McCrone, *Scotland's Future*, (Oxford: Blackwell, 1961).

[31] Cf. Second Report from the Expenditure Committee, *Regional Development Incentives* (H.M.S.O., January 1974).

[32] Wayland Kennet, Larry Whitty and Stuart Holland, *Sovereignty and Multinational Companies*, Fabian Tract (London, 1971).

[33] DATAR, *Investissements Entrangers et Aménagement du Territoire* (Paris: Livre Blanc, 1974) table 6.

[34] Maurizio Benetti, Mauro Ferrara and Corrado Medori, *Il Capitale Straniero nel Mezzogiorno* (Goines Edizioni, 1975) table 1. The authors do

not cite the precise date of the study, undertaken by SVIMEZ–ISSOCO, but state in their introduction that it was 'recent', and post 1970.

[35] DATAR, *Investissements Etrangers* pp. 18–21.
[36] Benetti, Ferrara and Medori, *Il Capitale Straniero*, pt III.
[37] John Firn, *External Control and Regional Policy*, in *The Red Paper on Scotland*, ed. Gordon Brown (E.U.S.P.B., 1975).
[38] See further Ibid. (1974) Minutes of Evidence, and Holland, *Multinational Companies and a Selective Regional Policy*.
[39] The detailed argument in support of the above case is available in Holland, *Capital versus the Regions*, ch.7.
[40] J. H. von Thünen, *Der Isolierte Staat in Beziehung auf Landwirtschaft und Nationalökonomie* (1826).
[41] See Robin Murray, 'Underdevelopment, International Firms and the International Division of Labour', in *Towards a New World Economy* (Rotterdam University Press, 1972). Basically this is a compilation of the conference proceedings, intro. Jan Tinbergen.
[42] See further Louis Turner, *Multinational Companies and the Third World* (Allen Lane, The Penguin Press, 1974).
[43] See further the I.B.M. case cited in the following chapter.
[44] After strike action at the Ford plant in Britain in 1970 Henry Ford II held a 'summit' meeting with the Prime Minister and delivered a press statement to the effect that 'we have got hundreds of millions of pounds invested in Great Britain and we can't recommend any new capital investment in a country constantly dogged with labour problems. There is nothing wrong with Ford of Britain but with the country.' Soon after, Ford shifted a £30 million operation for building Pinto engines from Britain to Ohio, and the following year announced that Ford's major new plant would be located in Spain, as a country which offered 'social peace'. Cf. Barnet and Müller, *Global Reach*, pp.308–9.
[45] Barnet and Müller, *Global Reach*, ch.11.
[46] See further Stuart Holland, 'European Para-Governmental Agencies', in Sixth Report from the Expenditure Committee, *Public Money in the Private Sector*, vol. III (1972).

Chapter 3

[1] Second Report to the Expenditure Committee, *Regional Development Incentives*.
[2] Ibid.
[3] Cf. Unilever's evidence in Second Report from the Expenditure Committee, *Regional Development Incentives*.
[4] Cf. I.B.M.'s evidence, ibid.
[5] 'Les aides à l'expansion industrielle régionale dans les pays du marché commun', *La Documentation Française*, Notes et études documentaires, no. 3917 (11 Sep 1972); Kevin Allen and Malcolm MacLennan, *Regional Problems and Policies in Italy and France* (London: Allen & Unwin, 1970).

⁶ Commissariat Général du Plan, *Essai de Régionalisation de l'Economie Française* (Nov 1964).

⁷ See, *inter alia*, Imprimerie Nationale, *Rapport sur l'Exécution du Plan en 1964 et 1965 et sur la Régionalisation du Budget d'Equipement de 1966* (1966) and La Documentation Française, 'Métropoles d'Equilibre et Aires Métropolitaines', *Notes et Etudes Documentaires*, no. 3633 (Nov 1969).

⁸ See further Chapter 5 and La Délégation à l'Aménagement du Territoire (DATAR), *Une Image de la France de l'an 2000 – Scénario de l'Inacceptable* (July 1971).

⁹ See further Holland, 'Regional Under-development in a Developed Economy'. For the Vanoni Plan see Ministero del Bilancio, *Schema di Sviluppo dell'Occupazione e del Reddito in Italia 1955–64* (1954).

¹⁰ Ministero del Bilancio, *Progetto di Programma di Sviluppo Economico per il Quinquennio 1965–69* (June 1964).

¹¹ Ministero del Bilancio, *Progetto di Programma di Sviluppo Economico per il Quinquennio 1966–70* (Jan 1965).

¹² See further Holland, 'Regional Under-development in a Developed Economy'.

¹³ A.J. Brown, *The Framework of Regional Economics in the United Kingdom*, p.xiii.

Chapter 4

¹ Jean Fourastié and J-P. Courthéoux, *La Planification Economique en France*, 2nd edn (Presses Universitaires de France, 1968) ch.2.

² Jean-Jacques Servan-Schreiber, *The American Challenge* (Harmondsworth: Penguin, 1970) first published as *Le défi américain*, (Paris: Denoel, 1967).

³ Cf. Pierre Uri, 'Harmonisation des politiques', *Révue Economique* (March 1958). Uri was a member of the sub-committee of the Spaak Committee which drafted the Rome Treaty proposals.

⁴ Cf. Bela Balassa, *The Theory of Economic Integration* (London: Allen & Unwin, 1962).

⁵ Cf. John Pinder, 'Problems of European Integration', in *Economic Integration in Europe*, ed. G.R. Denton (London: Weidenfeld & Nicolson, 1969).

⁶ Cf. Holland, 'Regional Under-development in a Developed Economy'.

⁷ See E.E.C. Commission, 'L'Evolution Régionale dans la Communauté', *Bilan Analytiqe* (1971) table 6.

⁸ Ibid. table 8.

⁹ The replacement investment proportion given by A.R. Kuklinski, *Criteria for the Location of Industrial Plant* (U.N. Economic Commission for Europe, 1967) is corroborated for the E.E.C. in the 1960s. Cf. E.E.C. Commission, *A Regional Policy for the Community* (1969).

¹⁰ von Neumann Whitman, 'International and Inter-regional Payments

Adjustment'; Alexandre Lamfalussy, *Investment and Growth in Mature Economies: the Case of Belgium* (London: Macmillan, 1961).

[11] Cf. Stuart Holland (ed.), *The Price of Europe: a Re-Assessment* (London: S.G.S.–Longmans, 1971). The productivity increases in manufacturing do not decisively demonstrate a 'stimulus' effect from the creation of the E.E.C., but are consistent with lagged benefits following the introduction of new large-scale plant with productivity-gaining techniques.

[12] E.E.C. Commission, *A Regional Policy for the Community*, p.34.

[13] See further, John Pinder, 'Problems of European Integration', in *Economic Integration in Europe*, ed. Denton.

[14] Cf. the argument of the first President of the E.E.C. Commission and ex-Foreign Secretary of West Germany, Walter Hallstein: 'Since Adam Smith the arguments in favour of free trade have been refined and qualified but the core of the theory still stands', in Hallstein, *United Europe: Challenge and Opportunity* (Oxford University Press, 1962) p.31. Hallstein has hardly modified his position in *Europe in the Making* (London: Allen & Unwin, 1972).

[15] R.A. Mundell, 'A Theory of Optimum Currency Areas', *American Economic Review* (Nov 1961).

[16] R.I. McKinnon, 'Optimum Currency Areas', *American Economic Review* (Sep 1963).

Chapter 5

[1] Part of this chapter was first circulated in a paper given by the author to the Urban Studies Conference at Christchurch, Oxford in autumn 1972.

[2] NE.E.C. Commission, *L'évolution régionale dans la Communauté* (1971).

[3] Ibid.

[4] E.E.C. Commission, *Social Statistics* (1970).

[5] Ibid. and U.K. Central Statistical Office, *Abstract of Regional Statistics* (1973).

[6] E.E.C. Commission, *Social Statistics*.

[7] Harold Lind and Christopher Flockton, *Regional Policy in Britain and the Six*, P.E.P.–Chatham House European Series, no.15 (Nov 1970).

[8] Holland, 'Regional Under-development in a Developed Economy'.

[9] See Avison Wormald, 'Growth Promotion: The Creation of a Modern Steel Industry', in *The State as Entrepreneur*, ed. Holland. This refusal by the Italian government followed a remarkably inept exercise on shipbuilding aids by the Commission's Competition Directorate, which wanted to harmonise and reduce government assistance to much lower levels than then or now offered by the Japanese government to shipbuilders. The Commissioner concerned brilliantly overlooked social cost–benefit analysis, international competition and national politics in one vain throw.

[10] E.E.C. Commission, *Premier Projet de Programme de Politique Economique à Moyen Terme* (Mar 1966).
[11] E.E.C. Commission, *A Regional Policy for the European Community*, (1969).
[12] I.R.I., *Annual Report* (1972) and Bank of Italy, *Annual Report* (1973).
[13] Cf. *Trade and Industry* (London: H.M.S.O., Apr 1975).
[14] See further Commons Expenditure Committee, *Regional Development Incentives*, Minutes of Evidence.
[15] See further, *inter alia*, Kevin Allen, 'Regional Intervention', in *The State as Entrepreneur*, ed. Holland.
[16] The Labour Party (i) 'The National Enterprise Board', *Opposition Green Paper* (1973) and (ii) *Labour's Programme* (1973). See also, Parti communiste français et parti socialiste, *Programme commun de gouvernement* (1972).

Chapter 6

[1] G.H. Borts and J.L. Stein, *Economic Growth in a Free Market* (Columbia University Press, 1964).
[2] Ibid. pp.3–4.
[3] Ibid. pp.207–9.
[4] Ibid. p.145.
[5] Ibid. pp.172, 179.
[6] Richard Austin Smith, *Corporations in Crisis* (New York: Doubleday, 1963).
[7] See J.G. Maddox *et al., The Advancing South: Manpower Problems and Prospects* (20th Century Fund, 1967) p.72, who not only point to the high capital costs in the machinery sector, but also point out that government defence and armaments expenditure stimulated both growth and profits in the sector during precisely the period Borts and Stein examine.
[8] Ibid. p.72. The Maddox data corroborates interregional industry and productivity disparity data for Italy in 1968. See further Holland, 'Regional Under-development in a Developed Economy'.
[9] Borts and Stein, *Economic Growth*, pp.207–8.
[10] For empirical evidence see Holland, *Capital versus the Regions*, chs 4 and 7.
[11] Kuznets and Rubin estimate net immigration to the United States to have totalled only 700,000 persons between 1820 and 1840, but 4,200,000 between 1840 and 1860, with the bulk of the flow from Ireland between 1846 and 1855. Simon Kuznets and Ernest Rubin, *Immigration and Foreign Born* (National Bureau of Economic Research, 1954). Italian immigration peaked later – the last quarter of the century – following the 'integration' of the North and South of the country from 1861–71.
[12] Cf. G.S. Callender, 'The Early Transportation and Banking Enterprises of the States in relation to the Growth of Corporations', *Quarterly*

Journal of Economics, vol. xvii (1902) pp. 125–6. Callender points out that the slave-system agriculture of the South was based almost exclusively on the production of cotton, sugar, tobacco and rice, and that slave owners found it cheaper to import both manufactures and temperate-zone food products from other regions, despite the fact that, before the rise of cotton farming they had previously produced wheat and cotton for export.

[13] This is one of the most complex issues in U.S. industrial growth on which there is a variety of opinion. Habakkuk points to the existence of money wages 30 per cent higher in the United States than in Britain in the 1850s, and Temin has located the evidence of visiting British industrialists that U.S. firms were employing absolutely more and technically more advanced machinery than they were themselves. Both authors take Robarth's argument that labour was expensive because of availability of inexpensive land and extend it by showing that this was only one factor, of which capital substitution under high demand and labour supply were others. See H.J. Habakkuk. *American and British Technology in the Nineteenth Century* (Cambridge University Press, 1962) pp.5 and 95; Peter Temin, 'Labour Scarcity in America', *Journal of Economic History* (Sep 1966) and E. Robarth, 'Causes of the Superior Efficiency of U.S.A. Industry as Compared with British Industry', *Economic Journal* (Sep 1946).

[14] For the 'ever rising level of the tariff' to 1828 see Stuart Bruchey, *The Roots of American Economic Growth 1607–1861* (London: Hutchinson, 1965) ch.5. For List's infant-industry case see Friedrich List, *National System of Political Economy.* A good survey of List's particular contribution can be found in Margaret E. Hirst, *Life of Friedrich List and Selections from his Writings* (New York: Kelley, 1970).

[15] Cf. L.E. Davis and J. Legler, 'The Government in the U.S. Economy, 1810–1902', *Journal of Economic History* (Dec 1966) p.815.

[16] Cole's analysis of regional prices shows major price variations which only began to align to any marked extent after the first quarter of the nineteenth century. Arthur H. Cole, 'Wholesale Commodity Prices in the United States 1700–1861', in *Capital Formation and Economic Growth,* ed. Moses Abramovitz (1955).

[17] Bruchey has drawn attention to 'a marked degree of regional specialisation, with the North-West concentrating its resources on the production of foodstuffs, the South-West on cotton, and the North-East on manufacturing. Income received from exports of cotton, mainly via New York City, played a leading part in making interregional interdependence possible. This income enabled the South to pay the North-East for manufactured goods.' Bruchey, *The Roots of American Economic Growth,* p.159. For an effectively identical analysis for the 1815–60 period see also Douglass C. North, *Growth and Welfare in the American Past* (Englewood Cliffs, N.J.: Prentice-Hall, 1966) p.78.

[18] Allan Boghe shows that interest rates of 17 per cent were being paid in Kansas in the 1870s, which gives an indication of the kind of profits which were earned at the time in order to encourage such debt-

repayment terms. Easterlin estimates that approximately 18 per cent of the total wealth of the six fast-growing central U.S. states of Minnesota, Iowa, Missouri, Nebraska, Kansas and Dakota Territory in 1880 was owned by capitalists outside the states themselves. This kind of return on capital and capital inflow could not be sustained with the relative decline of agricultural to industrial productivity over the longer term, but was enough to give a massive 'leg up' to the states concerned of a kind which they could not have secured through trying to improve agricultural productivity in an already heavily populated peasant region. See Allan Boghe, *Money at Interest* (University of Nebraska Press, 1955) pp.116–17, 272, and Everett Lee, Ann Miller, Carol Brainerd and Richard Easterlin, *Population Redistribution and Economic Growth* (The American Philosophical Society, 1957) pp.142–4. Lebergott's analysis of U.S. agricultural exports between 1860 and 1880 shows that 'American wheat had begun flooding into markets from Wales to Sicily, successfully competing with exports from Devon, Cawnpore and the Ukraine'; Stanley Lebergott, 'Labour Force and Employment 1800–1860', in *Output, Employment and Productivity in the United States after 1800,* National Bureau of Economic Research (1966). The reference to Sicily – one of the main regions of labour outflow towards the United States – gives an indication of the international dimension of the backwash effects from the internal spread effects of population and income generation in the United States itself.

[19] As Lebergott puts it: 'For the United Kingdom railways offered only a superior means of transport, competitive with existing roads and canals; for the United States they constituted the very condition for opening new territory, breaking into areas that had virtually no transport worthy of the name.' Ibid. p.121.

[20] Ibid., and Lebergott, 'United States Transport Advance and Externalities', *Journal of Economic History* (Dec 1966) pp.437–62 for the massively higher employment increases in construction, services and trade in the United States than in Britain during the 1860–80 period (the percentage employment increase in construction was four times that in Britain, and the services–trades increase five times the British increase). These indications of consequential investment and growth do not prove causality between the railways expansion and regional–national economic growth in the manner attempted by Fogel's inspired guestimates to four decimal places, but Fogel's analysis is limited precisely because of the extent to which he isolates railway construction from the multiplicity of other exceptional, self-reinforcing factors in U.S. economic growth during the nineteenth century. Cf. Robert W. Fogel, *Railroads in American Economic Growth: Essays in Econometric History* (Baltimore: Johns Hopkins Press, 1964).

[21] W.W. Rostow, *The Stages of Economic Growth* (Cambridge University Press, 1971).

[22] Vera Lutz, *Italy: A Study in Economic Development* (Oxford University Press, 1962).

REFERENCES 169

23 U.S. Bureau of the Census, 11th Census of the U.S. (1890) cited in North, *Growth and Welfare in the American Past*, p.141.

24 North, *Growth and Welfare*, p.142.

25 U.S. agricultural employment 'peaked' by 1910, but registered a 30 per cent increase from 1880 to 1910 against a 5 per cent decline in Britain. Lebergott, 'Labour Force and Employment 1800–1960'.

26 Cf., *inter alia*, Harlow Unger, 'IBM has all the odds in anti-trust case', *Guardian* (18 Oct 1972).

27 Borts and Stein, *Economic Growth in a Free Market*.

28 Gabriel Kolko, 'Max Weber on America: Theory and Evidence', *History and Theory*, 1, no.2 (1962) cited in Bruchey, *Roots of American Economic Growth*. Bruchey's excellent countervailance of the micro-myopic and pseudo-scientific econometric studies in U.S. economic history is well worth detailed attention.

29 Bernard Bailyn, *The New England Merchants in the Seventeenth Century*, cited in Bruchey, *Roots of American Economic Growth*.

30 Bruchey, *Roots of American Economic Growth* pp.128–30.

31 Callender, 'The Early Transportation and Banking Enterprises of the States', p.111.

32 Ibid. pp.132–3.

33 Ibid. p.153.

34 Lance E. Davis and John Legler, 'The Government in the American Economy 1815–1902, *Journal of Economic History* (Dec 1966) p.516.

35 Ibid. p.518.

36 Annals of Congress 1917–18, p.1377, cited in Callender, 'Early Transportation and Banking Enterprises'.

Chapter 7

1 See Averitt, *The Dual Economy*.

2 Perroux, 'La firme motrice dans la région et la région motrice', Actes du colloque international de l'Institut de Science Economique de l'Université de Liège (1961) reprinted in *L'économie du XXe siècle* (Presses Universitaires de France, 1964) ch.5. Perroux seems unaware of the extent to which his policy recommendation may necessitate locational controls.

3 Cf. *Industrial and Regional Development*, Cmnd. 4942 (London: H.M.S.O., Mar 1972) p.5.

4 See Brown, *Framework of Regional Economics*, p.277.

5 Nicola Cacace, *Informazioni SVIMEZ*, nos 23–4 (1970).

6 W.F. Luttrell, *Factory Location and Industrial Movement* (Cambridge University Press, 1962); I.R.I. Società Autostrade Ufficio Studi, *Primi Effetti Economici dell'Autostrada del Sole* (1965).

7 SVIMEZ, *La localizzazione industriale ed i costi sociale dell'insediamento di nuove unità lavorative* (Giuffre, 1957).

[8] For larger centres it might well be desirable to plan for a long-term reduction of population. This has been argued for Paris by both Pierre Dufau, *Non a l'Urbanisme* (Paris, 1964) and by J.F. Gravier, *L'Aménagement du Territoire et l'Avenir des Régions Franüaises* (Paris, 1964) p.160.

[9] Gardner Ackley and Luigi Spaventa, 'Emigration and Industrialisation in Southern Italy', *Banco Nazionale del Lavoro Quarterly Review* (June 1962).

[10] Olivier Guichard, *Aménager La France* (Paris, 1965) p.194.

Chapter 8

[1] See further Holland, 'Regional Under-development in a Developed Economy'.

[2] See Kevin Allen, 'Regional Intervention', in *The State as Entrepreneur*, ed. Holland.

[3] Holland (ed.), *The State as Entrepreneur*.

[4] See further, ibid. ch.12.

[5] The French in fact introduced the I.D.I. State Holding Company in 1970 with such an aim. But the holding so far has been too small to make a significant impact in areas other than motorway building and telephone communications. See further, Stuart Holland, 'European Para-Governmental Agencies', *Public Money in the Private Sector*, Sixth Report from the Expenditure Committee, vol. III (1972).

[6] See The Labour Party, 'The National Enterprise Board', *Opposition Green Paper* (1973).

[7] Department of Industry, *The Regeneration of British Industry*, Cmnd. 5710 (Aug 1974).

[8] See John Moore and Barry Rhodes, *Regional Development Incentives*, Memorandum, Second Report from the Expenditure Committee, (London: H.M.S.O., 1974).

[9] See further Holland (ed.), *The State as Entrepreneur*, chs 5 and 7, and I.R.I., *Annual Report* (1972).

[10] See 'State Entrepreneurship and State Intervention', in *The State as Entrepreneur*, ed. Holland, ch.1.

[11] Wider criteria for such planning are possible with comprehensive Planning Agreements of the kind already implemented in Belgium, and recommended for the Labour Government in Britain. See Stuart Holland, *The Socialist Challenge* (London: Quartet, 1975) ch.8.

[12] See William Alonso and Elliott Medrich, 'Spontaneous Growth Centers in Twentieth Century American Urbanisation', in *Growth Centers in Regional Economic Development*, ed. Niles M. Hansen (New York: The Free Press, 1972).

[13] For an outstandingly perceptive and cogently argued statement of the case for job dispersion in the United States see James L. Sundquist, 'Where Shall They Live', *Public Interest*, no.18 (1970).

[14] See William G. Shepherd, 'Re-Examining Public Enterprise', *Working Papers for a New Society*, vol.1, no.2 (1973).

[15] Callender, 'Early Transportation and Banking Enterprises'.

[16] John Kenneth Galbraith undoubtedly has done much to help expose this taboo in his recent *Economics and the Public Welfare* (Boston: Houghton Mifflin, 1974).

INDEX